# SCRAP SAVER'S
# Christmas Stitchery

## Sandra Lounsbury Foose

To Tracy, my surprise package!

Library of Congress Catalog Number: 85-61342
ISBN: 0-8487-0646-3
Manufactured in the United States of America
First Printing 1986

Executive Editor: Candace N. Conard
Production Manager: Jerry Higdon
Art Director: Bob Nance

*SCRAP SAVER'S CHRISTMAS STITCHERY*

Editor: Linda Baltzell Wright
Editorial Assistant: Lenda Wyatt
Copy Chief: Mary Jean Haddin
Designer: Viola Andrycich
Photographers: Jim Bathie, Beth Maynor,
  Courtland W. Richards, Sylvia Martin,
  Gary Clark, Katherine Adams

Special thanks to the following manufacturers for sharing their products:
Bias foldover tape by Talon-American, Inc.
Ribbon by C.M. Offray & Son, Inc.
Rickrack by Coats & Clark
Washable Rainbow ™ Felt by S.H. Kunin Felt Co.

# CONTENTS

# MAKING CHRISTMAS MEMORIES

*How quickly the Christmas season is upon us. Thanksgiving plans are made, Advent begins, and all of a sudden it's half-past December! At Christmastime, I always need more Christmas TIME! There's not even a moment to open one of those magazines that promise "The Very Best Christmas Ever."*

*Then in the midst of all this busyness, I remember that the miracle and the memories of Christmas are the true gifts of the season. So even if my own preparations aren't complete, Christmas is complete.*

*As you use this book of embellishments and begin your holiday plans, think about the miracle of that first Christmas, which really was "The Best Christmas Ever." It had everything—light, love, faith, family, friends, worship, hope, peace, joy, goodwill, sharing, affection, music, guests, gifts, and lots of surprises! All the ingredients were there for a perfect Christmas—all the things that we still need today to make beautiful Christmas memories.*

*This book is filled with some of my Christmas memories and many designs for you to make. But in a sense, the manuscript is unfinished, because I want you to tuck clippings and notes between the pages all through the year. Add ideas, poems, recipes, and such. Then, when you pull it out during Advent, it will be full of Christmas inspirations that will fall right into your lap!*

*Many of the designs involve hand sewing, so as you work, you can sit with your family instead of your sewing machine. To those who love you, your "presents" are not nearly as important as your "presence." That's the heart of Christmas.*

# IT'S BEGINNING TO LOOK A LOT LIKE CHRISTMAS

When does Christmas come to your house? How does the magic begin? Early in December you probably climb the attic stairs and search for those familiar boxes, filled with Christmas treasures and lots of memories. You unwrap the Nativity figures, and place a wreath on the door. Now it's beginning to look a lot like Christmas!

If you love to sew, it may begin to look a little like Christmas as early as June or July, when you pull out your patterns and start planning presents. And whether you start stitching in July or during the second week of December, the projects in this chapter will help you to create a cozy Christmas.

# PATCHWORK STOCKINGS

*Use these one-size-fits-all stocking patterns, and you will find that the variations are almost endless! Because the stocking is so large, each surprise you tuck inside can be individually boxed and gift-wrapped, adding an extra measure of anticipation and surprise.*

*The quilt blocks I've used as inserts are variations of the classic Pine Tree, Peony, Snow Crystal, and Star of Bethlehem patterns. If you would prefer to use another block, draw it on eight-to-the-inch or ten-to-the-inch graph paper in order to adapt it to the six-inch format.*

## QUILT BLOCK INSERTS

**1. Making the patterns**—Trace the pattern pieces listed for each individual block and paste onto cardboard. Be sure to include their grain lines. The broken lines of the patterns indicate the stitching lines.

**2. Marking and cutting the fabric**—Flip the patterns over and mark the back of the fabrics, using a sharp soft pencil and leaving at least ½" between pieces. Since there are no seam allowances on the patterns, add ¼" around each piece when you cut the fabrics.

**3. Sewing the blocks**—Stitch the seams by hand, following your pencil lines. Do not sew to the edge of the fabric. Lift intersecting seam allowances out of the way and sew under them to avoid lumps. Iron or finger-press seam allowances toward the darkest fabric.

**4. Finishing the stockings**—Complete Steps 1–6 of the stocking instructions, page 13.

## PINE TREE BLOCK INSERT
### Materials
Green print scrap, 8½" x 9½"
White or muslin scrap, 8¼" x 10"
Brown mini-dot scrap, 3" x 4"
Sewing thread: green, brown
Patterns: A, B, C, D, E, F, G

**1. Getting started**—Read the general directions for the Quilt Block Inserts.

**2. Cutting the fabrics**—From the green print, cut eighteen A triangles and one B triangle. From the muslin, cut eighteen A triangles, two C squares, one D triangle, one E patch, and one reversed E patch. From the brown mini-dot, cut one G and one F.

**3. Assembling the block**—Refer to Figure 1 and lay out the patches in that order on a flat surface. Start by stitching all the green print triangles to small muslin triangles, to create bi-colored squares. Then stitch the bi-colored

Figure 1: Assembling the Pine Tree Block

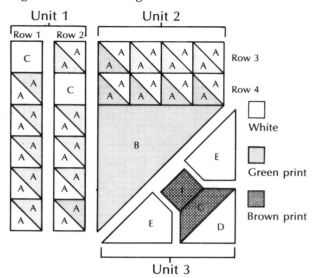

squares together into four rows, inserting a plain muslin square where indicated on the drawing.

Make three separate units. To create Unit 1, stitch together Row 1 and Row 2. To make Unit 2, join Row 3 and Row 4 and then

stitch the green print B triangle to the lower edge of Row 4. Start Unit 3 by stitching the brown dot G to one long edge of the brown dot F. Then stitch the muslin D triangle below the brown dot G. Arrange a muslin E piece at each side of the tree trunk and stitch.

Join Units 2 and 3 and then add Unit 1. Press the seams.

## FLOWER BLOCK INSERT
### Materials
Red-and-green floral scrap, 8″ x 12″
Green mini-dot scrap, 2½″ x 10″
Red scrap, 5″ x 10″
Sewing thread: red, green, white or natural
Green ⅛″ grosgrain ribbon, 12″
Patterns: H, I, J, K

**1. Getting started**—Read the general directions for the Quilt Block Inserts.
**2. Cutting the fabrics**—From the floral print, cut two H triangles, fourteen I squares, and fourteen J triangles for the background. Then use the K pattern to mark and cut ten green mini-dot diamonds for leaves and eighteen red diamonds for petals.
**3. Stitching the flower units**—Refer to Figure 2 and, on a flat surface, lay out the pieces for each quarter section of the main block, arranging three flower units and the leaf unit.

Stitch each of the individual flower units,

referring to the upper left portion of the drawing for guidance. Start by sewing two red petal diamonds together. Sew the remaining three pairs of diamonds together in the same way. Noting the placement of the red and green pieces in the drawing, join two pairs of diamond petals together to complete the all-red top half of the flower. Join the red and green units together to make the bottom half. Finger-press all the seams in the same direction. Pin the two flower halves together and sew from one end to the other, beginning on the pencil lines, not at the end of the fabric. Position the background print I squares and J triangles around each flower. Stitch one side of each petal to the adjoining square or triangle. Then stitch the remaining edges to complete each flower block unit. Repeat these directions to make three flowers.
**4. Stitching the leaf unit**—Refer to Figure 2 and join a green K diamond to each edge of a floral J triangle. Repeat to make another unit and then stitch the two units together. Add a floral I square to each inverted edge of the unit, stitching one side of each leaf to the adjoining square. Then stitch a floral H triangle to each edge of the unit.
**5. Assembling the block**—Stitch the two top flower units together. Stitch the remaining flower and leaf unit together, then join the two sections. Refer to the photograph and draw the stem lines, using a vanishing fabric marker. Cut pieces of the narrow grosgrain ribbon for the flower stems. Tuck under the cut ends and invisibly appliqué the ribbon to the patchwork. Start with the short stems and add the center stem last.

Figure 2: Assembling the Flower Block

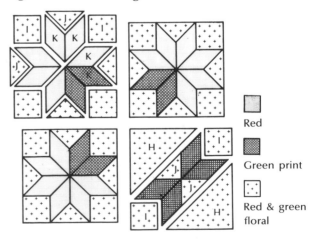

Red

Green print

Red & green floral

## SNOW CRYSTAL BLOCK INSERT
**Materials**
White-on-green mini-floral, 3½" x 7"
Green-with-white dot scrap, 4" x 10"
White or muslin scrap, 6" x 10"
Green-on-white mini-floral, 6" x 12"
Sewing thread: white or natural
Patterns: I, J, K, N

**1. Getting started**—Refer to general directions for the Quilt Block Inserts.
**2. Cutting the fabrics**—From the white-on-green floral print, cut eight I squares. From the green dot scrap, cut eight I squares, eight J triangles, and eight small N squares. From the white or muslin fabric, cut sixteen K diamonds. From the green-on-white floral print, cut sixteen K diamonds and eight N squares.

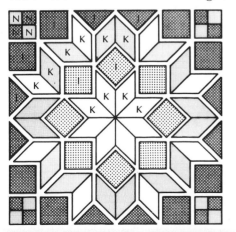

Figure 3: Assembling the Snow Crystal Block

| | |
|---|---|
| ☐ White | ▦ White-on-green print |
| ◩ Green-on-white print | ▩ Green-with-white dot |

**3. Assembling the block**—Refer to Figure 3 and lay out the patches in order on a flat surface. (This isn't a quick and easy project!)

Form the center of the snow crystal by stitching together eight white K diamonds, two at a time, to make four pairs. Then join two pairs together to form half of the crystal. Repeat to make another half and then stitch the halves together to make the entire crystal center. Add the white-on-green print I squares around the crystal edges, stitching one side at a time, on the pencil lines only.

Sew together pairs of the green-on-white print diamonds and the remaining white diamonds, referring to Figure 3 to determine their placement. At the center of each side and at each corner, the prints will be joined together. Stitch the diamond units around the snow crystal.

Add the I dotted squares and the J dotted triangles. Finally join the N dotted squares and N print squares and stitch these in place.

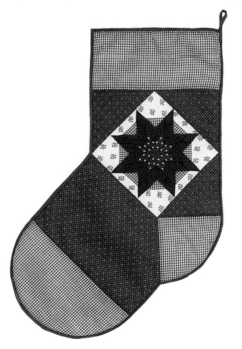

## STAR OF BETHLEHEM BLOCK INSERT
**Materials**
Green-with-white print scrap, 3½" x 10"
Red-with-white mini-dot scrap, 7" x 10"
Solid green scrap, 3½" x 10"
Green gingham (1/16" check), 3" x 9"
Red-and-green floral, 6" x 10"
Sewing thread: red, green
Patterns: J, K, L, M

**1. Getting started**—Refer to general directions for the Quilt Block Inserts.

**2. Cutting the fabrics**—Using the K pattern, cut eight green print pieces, sixteen red minidot pieces, and eight solid green pieces. Using the J pattern, cut eight green checked triangles. From the red-and-green floral scrap, cut four L pieces and four M pieces.

**3. Assembling the units**—Refer to Figure 4 and lay out the patches in order on a flat surface. Begin the block by stitching two diamonds together as shown on the left side of Figure 4. Refer to the drawing for color and print placement. Repeat the process to make sixteen pairs of diamonds. Then stitch two pairs together to make a large diamond consisting of four tiny diamonds. Again note the color and print placement in the figure. Form eight of these large diamonds in the same manner. To make Unit 1, stitch two large

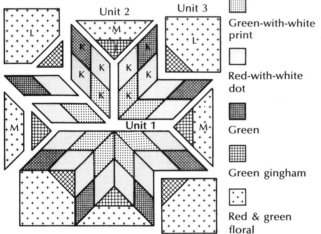

Figure 4: Assembling Star of Bethlehem Block

diamonds together (it will be formed of eight tiny diamonds). Repeat the process to make four Unit 1 pieces.

To make Unit 2, stitch a checked J triangle to a floral M piece. Make a total of four Unit 2 pieces.

Unit 3 is formed by stitching a checked green J triangle to the diagonal edge of a floral L piece. Make four Unit 3 pieces.

**4. Assembling the block**—Stitch together the two Unit 1 pieces to form half a star. Stitch the other two Unit 1 pieces together and then join the two halves. Position the Unit 2 and Unit 3 pieces around the star and stitch them in place, sewing only on the pencil outlines.

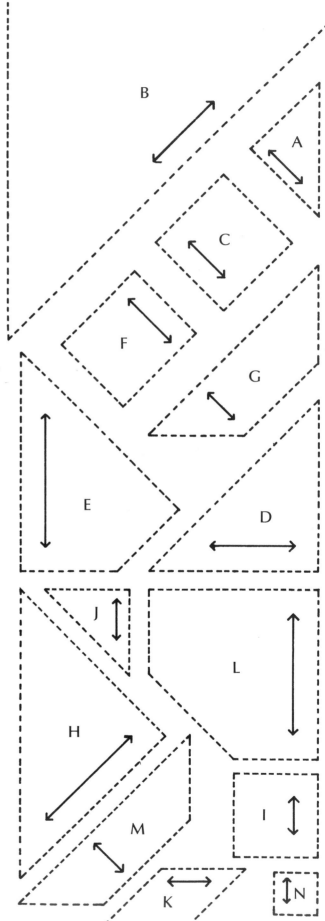

## STOCKINGS

### Materials

One completed quilt block insert (see individual quilt block inserts)
Print or plain fabric for front, 7" x 19"
Contrasting fabric for trim, 5½" x 24"
Print or plain fabric for backing, 15" x 24"
Print or plain fabric for lining, 24" x 30"
Quilt batting, 24" x 30"
Sewing thread to match fabrics and bias tape
Green ¼" fold-over bias tape, 2 yards

**1. Making the patterns**—Trace pieces O, P, Q, R, and S and their grain lines and paste them onto cardboard. The broken lines of the pattern indicate the stitching lines. Seam allowances must be added when you cut the fabrics. The completed stocking front will provide a pattern for the batting, the lining, and the back.

**2. Marking and cutting the fabrics**—Using a sharp soft pencil and leaving at least ½" between the pieces, flip the patterns over and draw the shapes on the back of the fabrics. When you cut the fabrics, add ¼" around each piece.

From the stocking fabric, cut three triangle O pieces and one shape P. From the contrasting trim fabric, cut one Q, one R, and one S. Do not cut the batting, the backing, or the lining at this time.

**3. Assembling the stocking front**—Refer to Figure 5 and attach an O patch to three sides of the quilt block insert, stitching only to the end of your pencil lines, not to the edges of the fabrics. Add the Q cuff, the P shape, the R toe, and the S heel. Press the seams.

**4. Preparing the remaining materials**—Use the completed stocking front as your pattern to cut the following pieces. First cut the batting and lining fabric in half crosswise, to make 15" x 24" pieces. On a flat surface, spread out the fabric for the back, right side down. Add a single layer of batting and top it with a piece of the lining fabric, right side up. Finally, place the completed stocking front on top, right side up. Pin all the layers together. Trim away the fabric and batting layers to match the stocking shape. Remove the completed stocking front and set it aside. Baste together all the remaining layers.

Spread out the remaining piece of lining fabric, right side down, and add a batting layer. Top the batting with the completed stocking front and pin and baste all the layers together. Trim away the fabric and batting layer to match the stocking front.

**5. Finishing the top edges**—Machine-stitch the layers together along the top edge of the stocking front, stitching ¼" from the edge. Then make a row of zigzag stitches, about ⅛" wide, within the seam allowance of the top edge. Next, trim away 1/16" of the seam allowance. Bind the top edge of the stocking front with the bias tape, using the machine stitches as a stitching guide. Prepare the top edge of the stocking back in the same way.

**6. Joining the front and back**—Pin and baste the stocking front to the back, with linings together. Machine-stitch around the stocking, stitching ¼" from the edge and leaving the top open. Then make a row of zigzag stitches, about ⅛" wide, within the seam allowance to flatten it. Next, trim away 1/16" of the seam allowance. Bind the edges of the stocking with the bias tape, extending the tape 4" beyond the top edge for a loop. Stitch together the open edges of the extended tape. Tuck in the cut end, form a loop, and tack it to the stocking back.

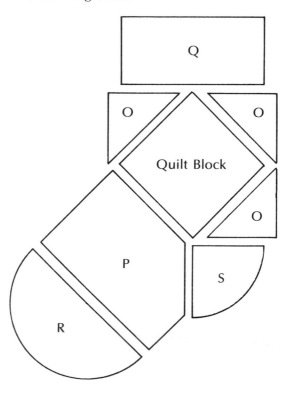

Figure 5: Assembling the quilt block stocking

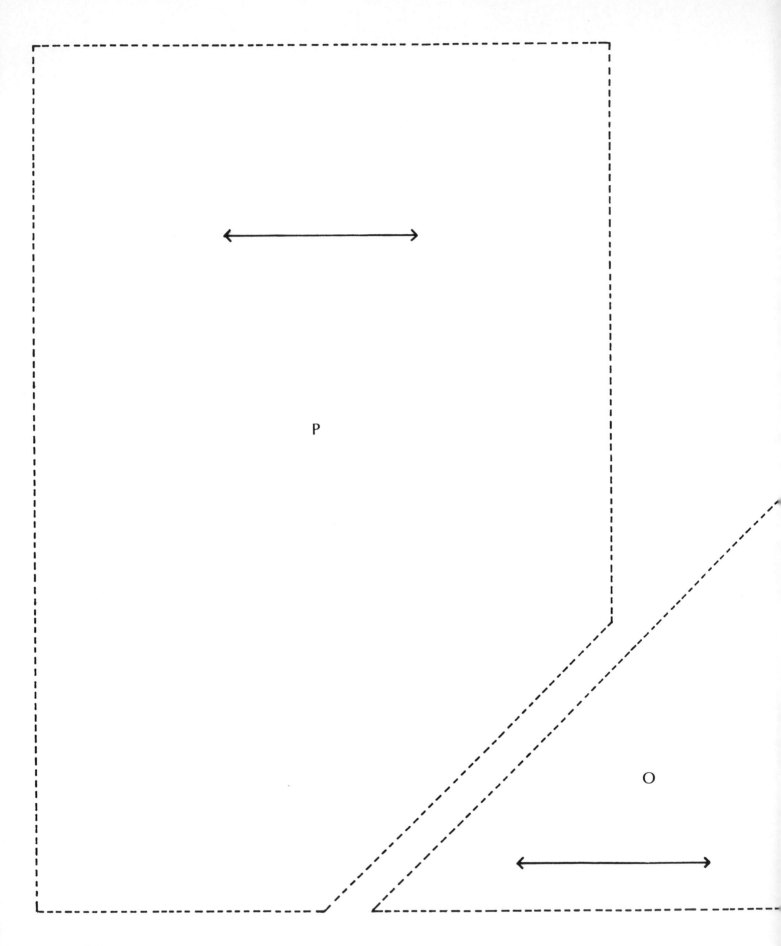

P

O

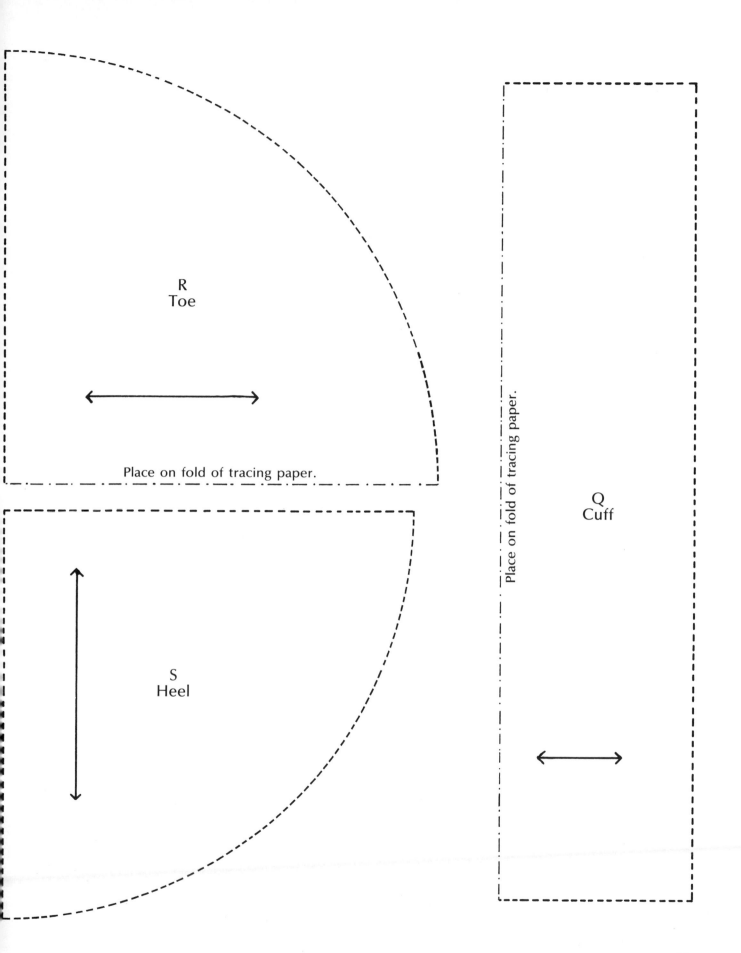

R
Toe

Place on fold of tracing paper.

S
Heel

Place on fold of tracing paper.

Q
Cuff

# ARGYLE LAP ROBE & STOCKING

*Simple patchwork squares and rickrack trims work together to imitate a traditional argyle knitting pattern. This quick-to-stitch lap robe and Christmas stocking inspire thoughts of a comfy chair and a cozy fire. Since the layers of the lap robe are tied together instead of quilted, you can just imagine how easy it is to make!*

*Stitched with deep red and green fabrics, these designs have a rich, somewhat masculine, personality, but with a change of palette, you could create a different story.*

## LAP ROBE
### Materials
White or muslin scrap, 20" x 28"
Dark green scrap, 16" x 30"
Red fabric, 45" x 49"
Dark green rickrack, medium width, 5 yards
White or natural rickrack, medium width,
  6 yards
Sewing thread: red, dark green
Solid or print fabric for backing, 45" x 45"
Quilt batting, 45" x 45"
Dark green embroidery thread, 1 skein
Dark green ⅞" quilt binding, 5⅛ yards

**1. Making the patterns**—Trace patterns A, B, and C for the lap robe, copying the matching dots and grain lines. Paste the patterns onto cardboard and cut them out. All the patterns include ½" seam allowances.

**2. Cutting the fabrics**—From the white scrap, cut four A triangles, four B triangles, and five C squares. From the dark green fabric, cut eight B triangles and four C squares. Refer to Figure 1 to mark and cut the red fabric, making sixteen C squares and four border pieces. The dimensions given for the border pieces include seam allowances.

**3. Arranging the patches**—After referring to Figure 2, lay out the patches in diagonal rows. Machine-stitch patches together, and press the seams open or to one side. Join the rows together.

**4. Adding the rickrack**—With a vanishing fabric marker or pencil, draw perpendicular lines through the center of each patch for the placement of the rickrack. Refer to the photograph and Figure 2 for guidance. The white rickrack will overlay the red and green patches. The green rickrack will overlay the red and white patches. Baste the white rickrack to the lap robe, or use fabric glue to hold it in place. Then machine or hand-stitch it right down the middle. Attach the green rickrack, overlapping the white rickrack.

**5. Adding the border pieces**—Pin and stitch the short border pieces to the top and bottom edges of the lap robe. If the border pieces are wider than the square, trim the ends to align. Pin and stitch the longer border pieces to the sides of the patchwork.

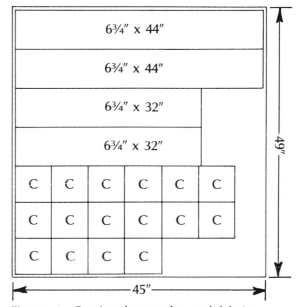

Figure 1: Cutting layout for red fabric

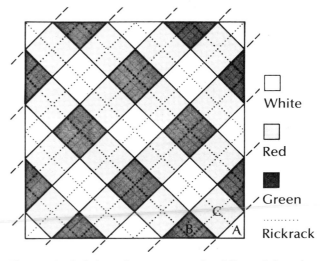

Figure 2: Joining the rows and adding rickrack

# ADVENT WINDOW BANNER

*Do you remember looking out your window on a starry winter night and wondering if Christmas would ever come? Stitch those memories into an Advent Window Banner, and you'll always be able to answer the question: "How many days?" I've used many traditional symbols of Christmas—peace and love, church and home, children and presents—to create twenty-four felt ornaments. The window panes on the banner are actually little pockets that hold the ornaments. So, every day of December, you can pull an ornament from its pocket. Each pocket is big enough to hold a special Advent message as well. This might be a sentence or two of the Christmas Story, or a hint that leads to a hidden surprise.*

## Materials
Felt, 8½″ x 11″ pieces: 4 red, 4 green
Iron-on fabric bonder, 19″ x 22″
Embroidery thread: 12 yards each of red, green
Navy-with-white star or dot fabric, 1⅝ yards
Quilt batting, 18½″ x 33″
White ½″ fold-over bias tape, 6 yards
White ⅞″ bias quilt binding, 3⅝ yards
Sewing thread: white, navy
White dressmaker pencil
18″ ruler or ¼″ wood slat, about 1″ wide

## ORNAMENTS
**1. Making the patterns**—Trace and cut each actual-size pattern, using a craft knife to cut out small areas like windows. If you plan to use these patterns several times, use quilter's acetate or paste your tracings onto flexible plastic or thin cardboard before you cut them out.

**2. Preparing the felt**—Cut the iron-on fabric bonder into four 8½″ x 11″ pieces. Make sandwiches of two same-colored pieces of felt with a layer of fabric bonder between.

Cut off a little corner of one of the sandwiches to use as a test patch. Experiment with time and temperature to find the best combination for bonding. Use a pressing cloth and avoid placing the iron directly on the bonding material.

**3. Cutting and stitching the ornaments**—Because felt is not a woven fabric, there are no grain lines, so you can turn the patterns and place them very close together. Draw around each shape, using a sharp soft pencil. From the red felt, cut one each: train, candy cane, house, bell, scissors, basket, reindeer, horn, bear, heart, airplane, angel. From the green, cut one each: cat, boy, snowflake, bird, girl, pig, star, car, tree, horse, camel, church.

Edge each ornament with tiny blanket stitches, using matching embroidery thread (2 strands).

## WINDOW BANNER
**1. Marking and cutting the fabric**—After referring to Figure 1, measure and draw the banner front, back, and the six pocket strips on the wrong side of the navy print fabric.

Figure 1: Marking and cutting the fabric

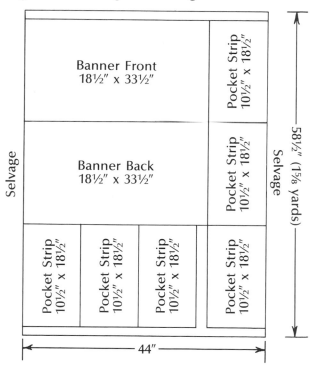

The dimensions include ½″ seam allowances, with an extra ½″ added to the lower edge of the front and backing pieces to allow for manufacturer's variations in the width of bias tape. (The extra fabric will be trimmed away in Step 4, if necessary.)

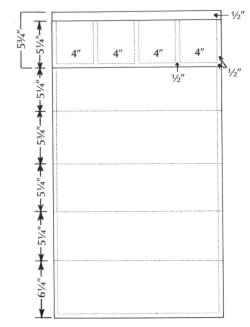

Figure 2: Pocket and bias tape placement

**2. Basting the layers together**—Place the banner front and back wrong sides together, with the batting in between. Baste all the layers together, ¼" from the edges.

Referring to Figure 2, label the top edge and then draw all the horizontal lines on the banner front, taking note that the placement lines for the pocket strips vary.

**3. Preparing the pocket strips**—Fold and press each of the six 10½" x 18½" navy pocket strips in half lengthwise, wrong sides together. After referring to the example in the first row of Figure 2, draw the lines on each folded strip, to indicate four pockets and bias tape placement.

First, prepare pocket strips for Rows 1, 2, 4, and 5. From the ½"-wide bias tape, cut four strips, each 18½" long. Baste these to each of the four pocket strips, encasing the lower cut edges and placing each tape on the guidelines you've drawn. Label each of the pocket strips. Reserve the remaining bias tape for the vertical strips.

For Row 3, cut one 18½" strip of the ⅞"-wide quilt binding. Baste it to the pocket strip, encasing the lower cut edges and placing the tape on the guidelines. Do not bind the pocket strip for Row 6.

**4. Stitching the pockets**—Again referring to Figure 2, start at the top of the banner, and pin and baste Row 1 in position. Place the

top folded edge of the pocket ½" below the top edge of the banner. Place the lower bound edge of the pocket directly on the first pocket placement line. Machine-stitch both edges of the tape in the same direction.

Add Row 2, placing its lower bound edge on the second placement line. The top folded edge of pocket strip 2 should be placed directly against lower edge of pocket strip 1.

Continue adding the pocket strips, remembering that pocket strip 3 is bound with the quilt binding, and pocket strip 6 is unbound. Trim below the final pocket strip so that the edges are even. Hand-baste around the side and bottom edges of the banner.

**5. Adding the vertical bias tapes**—From the ½"-wide bias tape, cut three pieces, each 33" long. Open only the center fold of one tape. Trim away about ¼" along one of the side folds, in order to create a flat ½"-wide tape with folds along each edge. Discard the trimmings. Trim the two remaining tapes.

Pin and baste each of the flat tapes in position on the front, to make the vertical window panes. Machine-stitch both edges of each tape to create the individual pockets.

**6. Binding the edges**—Use the quilt binding to encase the edges of the banner. Pin and baste the binding in place, mitering the tape at each corner. Machine-stitch the binding and then hand-stitch each mitered corner.

**7. Adding the support**—Cut five lengths of the ⅞"-wide bias tape, each 7" long. Fold one strip right side out to make a 3½" piece. Machine-stitch all edges. Overlap the ends about ¼" and hand-stitch them together to make a loop. Check to see if the loop will easily slide over the ruler or wood strip. Make adjustments if necessary. Make four more loops. Hand-stitch them to the banner back just below the top edge, spacing them at equal intervals. Insert the wood strip and flatten the loops to be sure they will not show above the top binding.

**8. Attaching the ornaments**—Place a pin in the center of the binding above each window pane. Cut twelve 6" lengths of the red embroidery thread and twelve 6" lengths of green. Stitch and knot one end of each piece of thread at the dot on the top of each ornament, and then stitch the other end of the thread at the pin. Adjust the length so that each ornament is centered in a pane.

Cut out.

Train

Reindeer

Pig

Horse

Cut out.

Cut out.

Cut out

Cut out.

Bell

Basket

Bear

Angel

Star

Tree

Airplane

Candy Cane

Horn

Cut out.

Bird

Car

Cut out.

Cut out.

Cut out.

Scissors

Cut out.

Cut out.

Cut out.

Church

Heart

House

Cut out.

Cut out.

Cut out.

Cut out.

Camel

Snowflake

Cat

Boy

Girl

# TREE TEA COZY

*In one of the churches where my husband served as pastor, several Scottish families were part of our congregation, and their gifts of shortbread at Christmas became a special tradition. Now we always have a taste of hot tea and shortbread on Christmas Eve and, of course, a wedge or two is saved for Santa. Even if he's late, this Christmas Tree Cozy will keep the teapot nice and warm for him.*

## Materials

Print 1: Green solid or mini-floral, 12" x 15"
Print 2: Green-with-white dot, 8" x 20"
Print 3: Green holly design, 10" x 19"
Print 4: Green tree motif, 12" x 19"
Print 5: Green floral, 14" x 19"
Washable white felt, 3" x 6"
Sewing thread: green, white
Thick quilt batting, 18" x 36" (or two thin pieces)
Solid or print for backing, 18" x 36"
Green ¼" fold-over bias tape, 77"
Silver metallic thread, 3 yards
Purchased silver star appliqué, 1" diameter

**1. Making the patterns**—Trace the patterns, copying all the matching dots and grain lines. Paste the tracing sheet onto cardboard and cut out each pattern. Since you need reversed patterns as well, avoid confusion and label both sides of each pattern, using a different-colored pencil for each side. Pierce each matching dot with a large needle.

**2. Marking and cutting the fabric**—Refer to individual patterns for the number and print fabric used for that piece. Mark the wrong side of each fabric and transfer all the matching dots by pushing a pencil into the holes. For accuracy, you should mark and cut each piece individually.

Cut the white felt into two 3" squares and draw the star shape on one. Baste this piece, right side up, to the remaining square, stitching within the star. Cut out the star.

**3. Stitching the units**—Referring to Figure 1, lay out pieces A–E and reverse pieces A–E. Stitch the pieces in each column to make two wedges, as illustrated. Press the seams in one direction.

Join the two wedges together to make a

**Figure 1: Stitching the units**

Reversed pieces

unit. Repeat this procedure to make a total of eight units. Stitch all the units together to form a large semi-circle.

**4. Adding the center top**—Stay-stitch the curved seam allowance of the F piece; then clip it almost to the stitching line at each dot. Pin and baste the F piece to the patchwork completed in Step 3, placing the right sides together. Match raw edges of patchwork and F piece, and align seams at dots. Press the back of the work so that the seam allowance of the F piece is flat.

**5. Attaching the layers**—On a flat surface, stack the layers as follows: backing fabric, right side down; batting; patchwork, right side up. Smooth out all the wrinkles and be sure that the long straight edge is truly straight. Pin the layers together and baste them about ³⁄₁₆" from the edges. Do not trim the excess batting and backing fabric yet.

Add extra pins within the patchwork area and hand or machine-quilt the zigzag lines between fabrics. Do not quilt around the semicircle F. The first line of stitching should be around the points of the A pieces.

When quilting is completed, remove pins and trim away the batting and backing.

**6. Completing the cozy**—Encase the lower pointed edges in bias tape, miter-

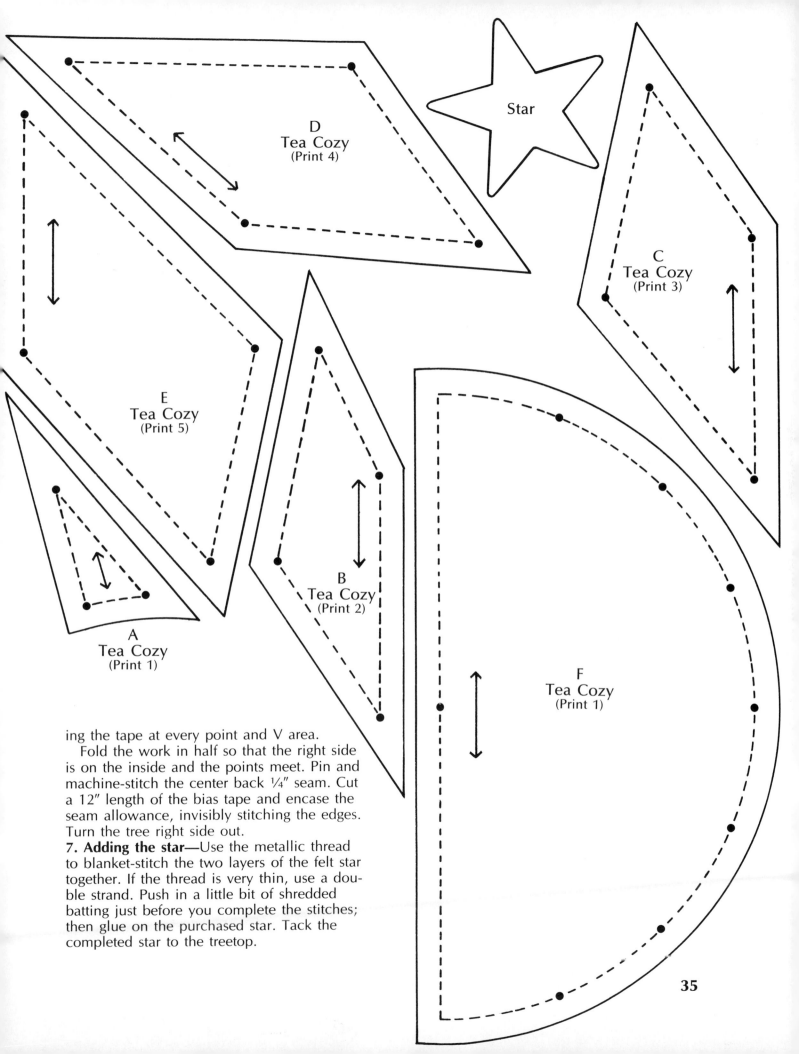

D
Tea Cozy
(Print 4)

Star

C
Tea Cozy
(Print 3)

E
Tea Cozy
(Print 5)

A
Tea Cozy
(Print 1)

B
Tea Cozy
(Print 2)

F
Tea Cozy
(Print 1)

ing the tape at every point and V area.

Fold the work in half so that the right side is on the inside and the points meet. Pin and machine-stitch the center back 1/4" seam. Cut a 12" length of the bias tape and encase the seam allowance, invisibly stitching the edges. Turn the tree right side out.

**7. Adding the star**—Use the metallic thread to blanket-stitch the two layers of the felt star together. If the thread is very thin, use a double strand. Push in a little bit of shredded batting just before you complete the stitches; then glue on the purchased star. Tack the completed star to the treetop.

35

# PATCHED WREATHS

*This project started as a drawing for a quick-to-stitch place mat. Then it seemed like a good idea for a pot holder and—why not add some stuffing to the patches and create a wreath, I thought! When that was done, the square patches invited some more detailed patchwork, and a galaxy of stars was added to the wreath. It was the beginning of a never-ending story!*

*Hmmm, now let's see. If I just enlarge these patterns a little more and add some patches to the center, I could make a tree skirt, and then . . .*

## PLACE MAT & POT HOLDER

**Materials for one place mat** *(15" x 15")*
Green print, tiny floral, 9½" x 11"
Green print, medium floral, 9¾" x 14¼"
Opaque white scrap, 8½" x 9¼"
Fabric scrap for backing, 16" x 16"
Quilt batting, 16" x 16"
Green ¼" fold-over bias tape, 50"
Sewing thread: white, green, red
Red ⅝" grosgrain ribbon, 21"

**Materials for one pot holder** *(8⅛" x 8⅛")*
Green-and-white dot scrap, 6" x 7"
Green gingham (⅛" check), 3¼" x 18"
Opaque white scrap, 5¼" x 5¼"
Fabric, preferably Teflon-coated, 9½" x 9½"
Quilt batting, 9½" x 19"
Green ¼" fold-over bias tape, 30"
Sewing thread: white, green, red
Red ¼" grosgrain ribbon, 9"
White all-purpose plastic ring, ⅝" diameter

**1. Making the patterns**—Trace, label, and copy the grain lines, the matching dots, and the ribbon placement lines for the patterns. Cut them out and pierce the matching dots and placement lines with a pin or needle. The patterns include a ¼" seam allowance.

**2. Marking and cutting the fabrics**—Note the grain lines on the patterns and then mark the back of the proper fabrics. For the place mat, draw six tiny floral A triangles and six medium floral B squares. Place the C pattern on the folded white fabric and mark one hexagon. For the pot holder, use the green dot fabric for A, the checked fabric for B, and the white for C. Indicate the matching dots on the back of the patches by making a pencil dot at each pin hole. Lightly transfer the ribbon placement lines to the front of only one of the B squares, using a vanishing fabric marker. Cut out the patches.

**3. Assembling the wreath**—Using Figure 1 as a guide, join all the triangles and squares, right sides together, alternating the patches and making a ring. Stitch the seams from dot to dot, backstitching at the start and finish.

Add the white hexagon to the center of the ring, pinning and stitching one side at a time and backstitching at the start and finish of each seam.

**4. Adding the batting and backing layers**—For the pot holder, cut the batting in half to make two 9½" squares. Use both layers of batting for extra thickness. For the place mat, use a single layer of batting.

Stack the backing fabric right side down and the wreath right side up with the batting between. Pin and baste the layers together, but don't do any trimming yet. Quilt by hand or machine around the center white hexagon patch and between each square and triangle. (I quilted right on the seam line.)

**5. Finishing the edges**—Baste a line of hand stitches around the wreath, ⅛" from the edge. Next, machine-stitch around the wreath, ¼" from the edge. Trim away a little more than 1/16" of the wreath seam allowance close to the line of hand stitches, cutting the batting and backing layers, too.

By hand or machine, stitch bias tape around the edge, easing the tape around each point.

**6. Adding the bow**—For the place mat, cut the ⅝" ribbon into four pieces. Cut a 1¾" center, an 11" piece for loops, and two ends, each 3¾" long. For the pot holder, use the ¼" ribbon and cut a 1" center, a 5⅝" piece for loops, and two ends, each 1⅞" long.

Pin the two end pieces in place, folding under one cut end of each and invisibly stitching all the edges to the wreath. Next, fold the loop piece, pin in position, and stitch. Finally, add the center, tuck under each cut end, and then stitch it in place.

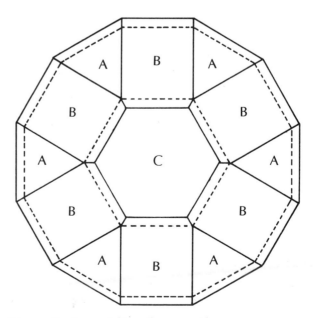

Figure 1: Assembling the wreath

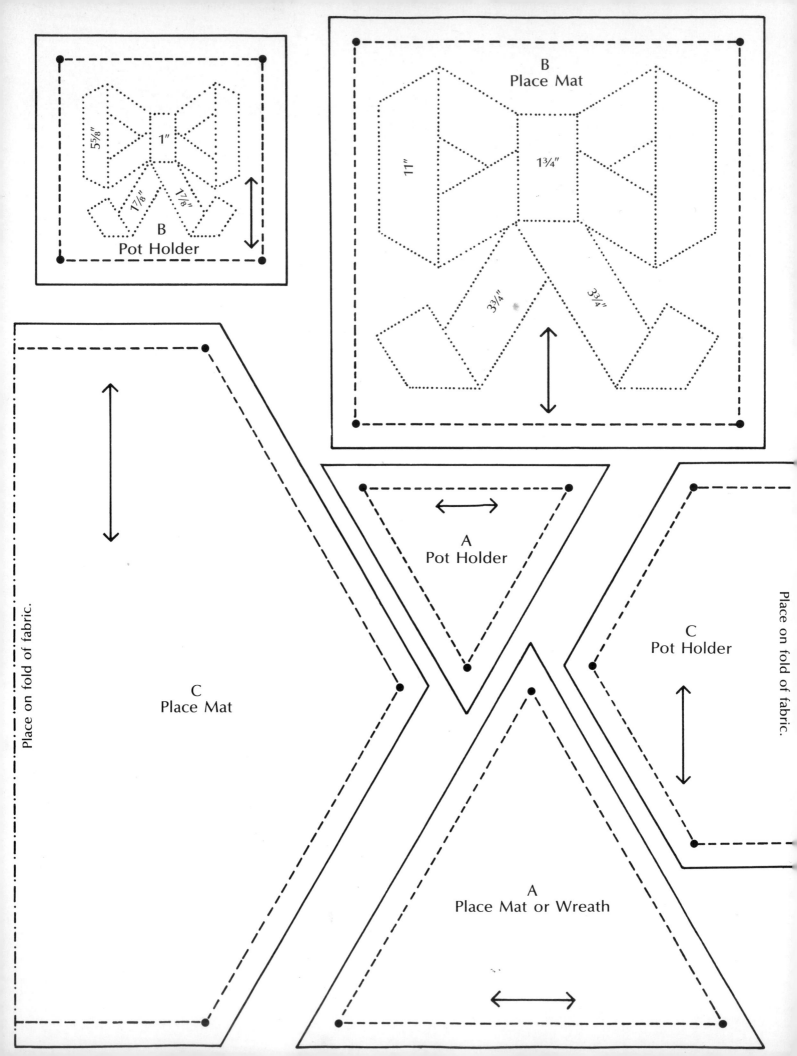

B
Place Mat

5⅝"

1"

B
Pot Holder

1⅞"    1⅞"

11"    1¾"

3¾"    3¾"

A
Pot Holder

C
Place Mat

Place on fold of fabric.

C
Pot Holder

Place on fold of fabric.

A
Place Mat or Wreath

# WREATH
## Materials
Green floral scrap, 4½" x 18"
Green-with-white dot scrap, 4½" x 6½"
Ecru-with-green print, 4½" x 34"
Opaque ecru scrap, 4½" x 12"
Green scrap, 4½" x 24"
Scrap for backing, 16" x 16"
Polyester stuffing
Green ¼" fold-over bias tape, 2¼ yards
Sewing thread: ecru, green
One ring of 10"-diameter embroidery hoop

**1. Making the patterns**—Trace, label, and copy the grain lines and the matching dots for wreath patterns A, D, and E. Cut them out and pierce the matching dots with a large needle. The patterns are actual size and include ¼" seam allowances.

**2. Marking and cutting the fabrics**—Cut out the patches, transferring all the matching dots and grain lines. From the green floral fabric, cut six large A triangles. Using pattern D, cut six squares from the green dot scrap and twenty-four squares from the ecru-with-green print. Using pattern E, cut twenty-four ecru triangles, twenty-four ecru-with-green print triangles, and forty-eight green triangles.

**3. Stitching the star blocks**—Refer to Figure 2 and lay out the patches in order for one star block. Join the small triangles together, two at a time. Sew these larger triangles together to make four units. Then stitch these units to the D squares to make three horizontal rows as shown in Figure 2. Finally, join the three

rows together to make a complete star block B. Press the seams open or towards the darkest fabric. Repeat the procedure to make a total of six blocks.

**4. Assembling the wreath front**—Lay out the pieces on a flat surface, using the photograph and Figure 1 on page 37 as a guide. Join all the A triangles and star blocks, right sides together, alternating the pieces. Carefully check the grain lines of the triangles and place these patches so that the straight grain will be on the outside edge of the wreath. Stitch the seams from dot to dot, backstitching each seam at the start and finish. Press seams to one side.

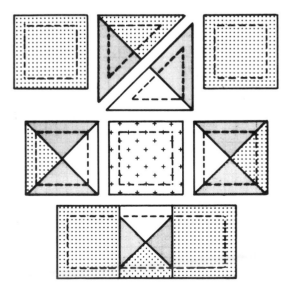

Figure 2: Assembling Star Block B

**5. Adding the backing**—Pin the completed wreath front to the backing fabric, wrong sides together. Don't trim away the backing at this time. Machine-stitch the center of the wreath on the stitching line, ¼" from the cut edges.

Machine-topstitch each triangle seam. Begin stitching at the outside edge of the wreath and sew toward the center. At the tip of each triangle, lift the machine presser foot. Leaving the needle in the fabric, rotate the work so that you can pivot the stitching line. Continue stitching toward the outside edge of the wreath. Backstitch at the start and finish of each line. Leave the entire outside edge of the wreath open for stuffing.

Now carefully trim away the excess backing around the center and the outside edges, leaving the ¼" seam allowances.

**6. Stuffing the wreath**—Stuff each little pocket around the wreath, pushing the stuffing into the corners with a crochet hook or a blunt pencil. Stuff all the squares first and then go back and do all the triangles. Flatten the wreath as you work.

Close the openings around the wreath with pins placed perpendicular to the edges. Hand-baste ⅜" from the edges, so that there will be room for the machine's presser foot. Machine-stitch around the outside, ¼" from the edges. Remove the pins and basting stitches. Trim away ¹⁄₁₆" of the seam allowance around the outside and inside of the wreath. If necessary, redistribute the stuffing with a long needle.

**7. Finishing the edges**—Check the center of the wreath and, if the fabric puckers at the tip of each triangle, clip out some of the extra seam allowance, but avoid cutting the stitches.

Encase the outside edges in bias tape, invisibly hand-stitching it first to the front and then to the back. Ease the tape around the corners.

Encase the edges of the center opening in bias tape, making a tiny pleat at each inside corner and invisibly tacking it in place.

**8. Adding the support**—Attach the embroidery hoop to the back of the wreath. Stitch a piece of thread at the center back of each square and triangle section and tie the thread around the hoop.

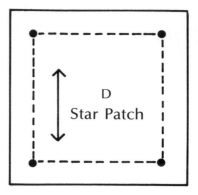

D
Star Patch

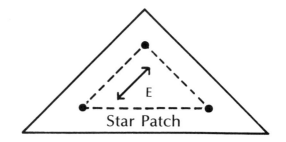

E
Star Patch

# CRÈCHE

This soft Nativity Scene symbolizes the very heart of Christmas love. The barn door folds down to create a meadow and to reveal the Holy Family, a visiting Angel, and assorted sheep and lambs. The Angel and the lambs can be made individually as ornaments for your tree. The sides of the barn are made with peek-in windows, and both the interior and the meadow are large enough to accommodate the entire cast of characters. You can even make additional figures—shepherds, kings and such—using the basic patterns.

Although the crèche is unbreakable and invites little hands to touch, some of the tiny pieces used for the lambs and the Baby make the set unsuitable for unsupervised play by children under three.

**STANDING FIGURES**
**Materials for Mary**
Pink felt, 3½" x 6½"
Blue floral scrap, 5" x 16"
Blue scrap, 8" x 11"
Lightweight cardboard, 3" x 3"
Sewing thread: pink, blue, cream
Polyester stuffing
Embroidery thread: 18" each of dark brown, medium pink, light pink; 1¼ yards blue; 11 yards auburn
Pipe cleaner, 6"
Pregathered narrow cream lace, 1 yard

**Materials for Joseph**
Pink felt, 3½" x 6½"
Brown mini-print, 5" x 16"
Unbleached muslin, 8½" x 10"
Lightweight cardboard, 3" x 3"
Sewing thread: pink, tan, cream
Polyester stuffing
Embroidery thread: 18" each of dark brown, medium pink, light pink; 2¼ yards dark tan; 11 yards dark brown
Pipe cleaner, 6"

**Materials for Angel**

Pink felt, 3½" x 6½"

Cream print, 5" x 16"

Unbleached muslin, 8½" x 8½"

Quilt batting, 5" x 8½"

Lightweight cardboard, 3" x 3"

Cream sewing thread

Polyester stuffing

Embroidery thread: 18" each of dark brown, medium pink, dark pink; 1¼ yards peach; 11 yards light brown

Pipe cleaner, 6"

Pregathered narrow cream lace, 18"

Flat, narrow cream scalloped lace, 26"

42

**1. Making the patterns**—Trace and label the actual-size patterns on pages 44 and 45. Pierce the features and the placement lines with a large needle. Mark the quarter sections on the body and the base. Seam allowances are included on all the pieces: ⅛" on the head, and ¼" on all the other pieces.

**2. Cutting the fabrics**—For each standing figure, draw and cut out one head and four hands on the pink felt. Lightly transfer the facial features, by pushing a sharp soft pencil into the needle holes in the pattern. Also transfer the dotted line below the mouth, indicating the placement of the head on the body, and the dotted line above the eyes that is the center part line for the hair. For each body, cut one cardboard base.

MARY—From the blue floral fabric, cut one body, one base, and two arms. Fold the plain blue fabric in half crosswise. Place the cloak pattern on the fold where indicated, and cut out. Cut two cloaks in this manner.

JOSEPH—From the brown print, cut one body, one base, and two arms. Fold the muslin in half crosswise. Place the head-covering pattern on the fold where indicated, and cut two head coverings. Transfer the gathering line to one piece.

ANGEL—From the cream print, cut one body, one base, and two arms. Using the unbleached muslin, cut two wings and two halos. Lightly transfer the embroidery lines. Cut a wing and halo circle from the batting.

**3. Stitching the body**—Stitch the center back seam of the body with the right sides together. Flatten the cone so that the center back seam meets the center front marking. Stitch across the shoulder seam (top edge). Turn right side out, and mark the seam allowance along the lower edge. Turn the seam allowance to the inside and baste it in place. Stuff the body firmly.

Mark the seam allowance around the base, turn it under, and baste in place. Push the cardboard base into the stuffed body and cover it with the fabric base, matching the quarter sections. Slipstitch the edges together.

**4. Forming the head**—Using a strong doubled thread, make a row of running stitches around the head, ⅛" from the edge. Pull both ends, slightly gathering the circle. Place tight wads of stuffing inside the head. Pull the gathering thread very tightly and knot. The opening at the back of the head should be only about ⅝" wide. Flatten the head so that it is approximately 1½" wide. Add more stuffing through the opening, so that very little puckering is visible when you look at the front of the head. All around the edges of the back opening, make a web of stitches from one side to the other, to reinforce it.

Embroider the facial features, using one strand of embroidery thread. Use satin stitches or French knots for the dark brown eyes. Use medium pink satin stitches for the cheeks and pink backstitches for the mouth. Invisibly stitch the head to the body.

**5. Styling the hair**—

MARY—Cut off an 18" length of the auburn embroidery thread and reserve it for stitching the hair to the head. From the remaining thread, cut off eighteen pieces, each 8" long, for the braid.

Cut all the leftover thread into 6" lengths (6 strands) and stitch these lengths to the head. Several pieces can be added at one time. The center of each piece of embroidery thread should be stitched to the head at the center part, using a single strand of matching thread. Overlap the pieces of hair so that no pink felt shows through. Gently drape the hair down slightly towards the neck and towards the back. Tack it there. Since the back of the head will eventually be hidden by Mary's blue cloak, you don't need to worry about how it looks.

To make the braid, use a piece of thread and tightly tie together the eighteen 8" lengths of reserved embroidery thread. Tape or pin the combined threads to your work surface and loosely braid them together. Keep the braid rather flat and about ⅜" wide. Use another piece of thread to tightly join the ends. Securely wrap the braid around the lower part of the head, tacking it near the top and draping it down behind the neck area. Add a few loose stitches to attach the braid to the hair.

JOSEPH—Follow the directions for MARY, using dark brown thread. Add the braid as a beard, before you tack the hair to the back of the head. The hair should drape over the beard at the sides.

ANGEL—Follow the directions for MARY, using light brown thread and crowning the top of the head with the braid.

**6. Making the arms**—Stitch a felt hand to each end of each arm and press the felt seam allowance toward the fabric. Pin the two arm sections, right sides together, and machine-stitch around the unit, leaving a 2″ opening along the center of the straight edge. Trim the seam allowance around the hands to ⅛″ and carefully clip the curves. Turn the piece right side out, poke out the hands, and flatten the unit but do not stuff it.

Fold back about ¾″ of each cut end of the pipe cleaner and insert it within the arm unit, making sure the pipe cleaner enters the hands. Slipstitch the sleeve opening closed. Center the arm unit on the back of the body and tack it in place.

Add the pregathered lace trimming to the neck, sleeves, and hem of the dresses of Mary and the Angel.

**7. Braiding the waist cord**—For Mary and the Angel, cut three 14″ lengths of embroidery thread (6 strands), and for Joseph cut three 12″ lengths. For each braid, knot the lengths together, leaving a ¾″ tassel of loose threads at the end. Tape the knot to your work surface and tightly braid the strands. Leave about 1″ of the threads unbraided and knot the ends together, leaving a ¾″ tassel. Use

blue thread for Mary, peach for the Angel, and dark tan for Joseph. Tie a cord around the waist of each standing figure, making a bow for Mary and the Angel and a knot for Joseph. Tack the cord at the center back and front.

**8. Adding the finishing touches**—

MARY—To make the cloak, stitch the center back seam of each folded piece. Machine-stitch a ¼″ seam, stopping at the dot on the top fold line. Trim and clip the seam; then press the seam open or to one side. Cup one cloak inside the other, right sides together. Pin and then stitch the edges, leaving about 1½″ open for turning. Turn the piece right side out and slipstitch the opening closed. Press the piece so that the seam is exactly on the edge. Baste around the edge and then trim it with lace. Glue or tack the cloak in place.

JOSEPH—Refer to the directions for Mary's cloak to make the unbleached muslin head covering. Instead of lace, add a row of dark tan running stitches. Using embroidery thread (2 strands), place the stitches about ⅛″ from the edge.

With cream sewing thread, make a line of running stitches around the oval placement

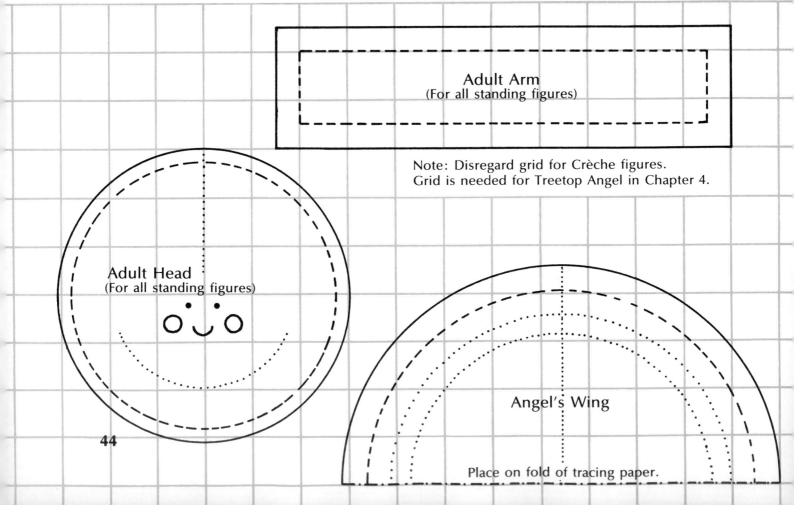

Adult Arm
(For all standing figures)

Note: Disregard grid for Crèche figures.
Grid is needed for Treetop Angel in Chapter 4.

Adult Head
(For all standing figures)

Angel's Wing

Place on fold of tracing paper.

44

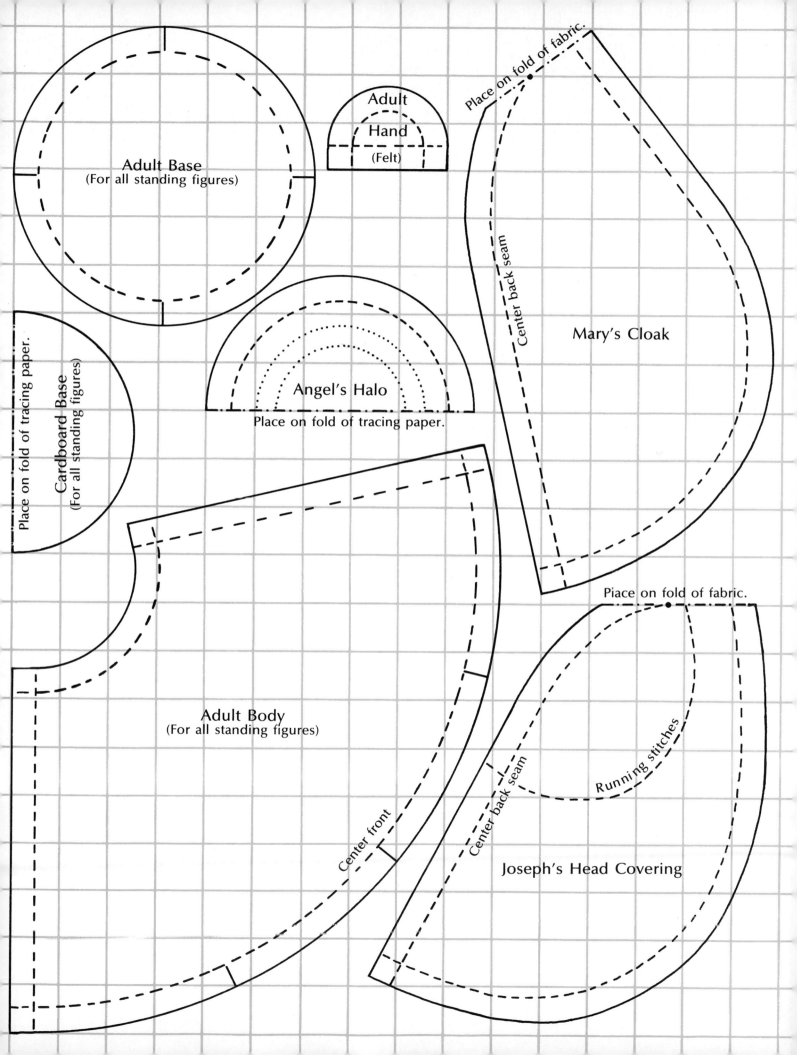

Adult Base
(For all standing figures)

Adult
Hand
(Felt)

Place on fold of fabric.

Center back seam

Mary's Cloak

Place on fold of tracing paper.

Cardboard Base
(For all standing figures)

Angel's Halo

Place on fold of tracing paper.

Piace on fold of fabric.

Running stitches

Adult Body
(For all standing figures)

Center front

Center back seam

Joseph's Head Covering

line on the head covering. Pull the stitches, fitting the head covering to the head and tacking it in place.

Make a braid for a headband, using three 14″ lengths of dark tan embroidery thread. Tie the headband in place, covering the running stitches.

ANGEL—Layer the halo circles in the following order: batting; unmarked circle, right side up; marked circle, right side down. Hand-baste the layers together, ⅛″ from the edge. Machine-stitch ¼″ from the edge, leaving about 1″ open for turning. Clip the curves, but don't clip the seam allowance at the opening. Remove the basting and turn the circle right side out. Tuck under the edges of the opening and stitch closed.

Flatten the edges of the halo to make it as perfect a circle as possible. Be sure that the seam line is exactly on the edge. Hand-baste around the halo, close to the edge. Using blue embroidery thread (2 strands), make a row of running stitches around the halo. Make a second row, using the peach-colored thread. Trim the edge with scalloped lace.

Refer to the halo directions to make the larger circle for the wings. When completed, softly fold the circle in half and machine-stitch it from the center of the fold down to the outside edge. Tack the wings to the Angel's back along the machine-stitching line.

## BABY JESUS
### Materials
Pink felt, 2″ x 7″
Polyester stuffing
Sewing thread: pink, blue, cream
Embroidery thread: 12″ each of dark brown,
   medium pink, dark pink; 1½ yards blue
Cream ½″ fold-over bias tape, 6″
Blue fabric, 4″ x 8″

**1. Drawing the patterns**—Trace and label the head and body patterns. Pierce the facial features with a pin. The pattern lines are the cutting lines for all the pieces. There are no patterns for the bunting or the blanket.

**2. Cutting the felt**—Draw one face and one body on the pink felt. Lightly transfer the facial features by pushing a sharp soft pencil into the pin holes on the face pattern.

**3. Stitching the body**—Fold back ¼″ of one short end of the body and stitch it in place. Using this edge as the starting point, roll up the strip tightly to create a little cylinder. Stitch down the free end of the strip. To form shoulders, decrease one end of the cylinder by making stitches from front to back and side to side and pulling them tightly. The opposite end of the cylinder should be flattened and stitched tightly.

**4. Forming the head**—Refer to Step 4 of the general directions for the Standing Figures. The opening at the back of the baby's head should be about ¼″ wide, and the head itself should be about ⅝″ wide. After embroidering the face, stitch the head to the shoulders.

**5. Making the bunting**—Open the center fold of the bias tape and iron it flat. Cut a 2½″ strip for the cap and reserve the remaining piece for the bunting.

Open one of the remaining folded edges of the cap strip, press it flat, and bring this cut edge towards the cut edge of the remaining fold, so that they meet. Press the tape again. The bias strip should be about ¾″ x 2½″.

Wrap this adjusted tape around the baby's head and invisibly stitch one folded edge around the face. At the back of the head, make a row of tiny running stitches, right on the folded edge of the tape. Pull the stitches to gather the bonnet back. Pull the front edge of the bonnet forward around the face so that the edge is very softly rolled. Add a little stuffing inside the back of the bonnet, if necessary. Wrap thread around the bonnet neck area and secure it.

To make the lower portion of the bunting, use the remaining 3½″ piece of bias tape and open all the folds so that it is about 1⅜″

Baby Body Strip
(Felt)

Baby's Head
(Felt)

wide. Fold the strip crosswise, with the right side on the inside, and machine-stitch each 1¾" side, using each flattened fold line as a seam guide. Turn the unit right side out and fold under ¼" of the cut edge of the top opening. Slip the bunting on the baby's body and add running stitches along the top fold. Pull the stitches to gather the edge, and knot the thread.

Wrap a 12" piece of blue embroidery thread (6 strands) around the back of the neck, cross it over the chest, wrap it around the back of the body, and then bring it to the front and knot.

**6. Making the blanket**—Cut the blue fabric into two 4" squares. Pin the right sides together and machine-stitch a ¼" seam around the outside edge, leaving about 1½" open along one side for turning. Clip off the corners and turn the blanket right side out. Press the blanket and baste around it, making sure that the seams are precisely on the edges. Trim the edges with blanket stitches or running stitches using blue embroidery thread (2 strands). Wrap the baby in the blanket.

**MANGER**
**Materials**
Beige felt, 4" x 9"
Cream felt, 1½" x 2½"
Embroidery thread: 18" cream, 1 yard beige

**1. Making the patterns**—Trace the patterns for the manger. Copy all the placement dots. All the pattern lines are cutting lines.
**2. Cutting the felt**—From the beige felt, cut two manger side pieces and four end pieces. Copy the placement dots on both side pieces and two of the end pieces. On paper such as stationery, draw and cut out one side insert piece and two end insert pieces. From the cream felt, cut two heart appliqués.
**3. Stitching the manger**—To prepare the side piece, baste together the two felt layers along the notched edges only, with the placement dots on the outside. Blanket-stitch the notched edges, using beige embroidery thread (2 strands). Remove the basting stitches and slip in the paper insert. Baste the straight edges together to encase the paper.

To prepare each end piece, appliqué a cream heart to one of the beige ends, blanket-stitching with cream embroidery thread (2

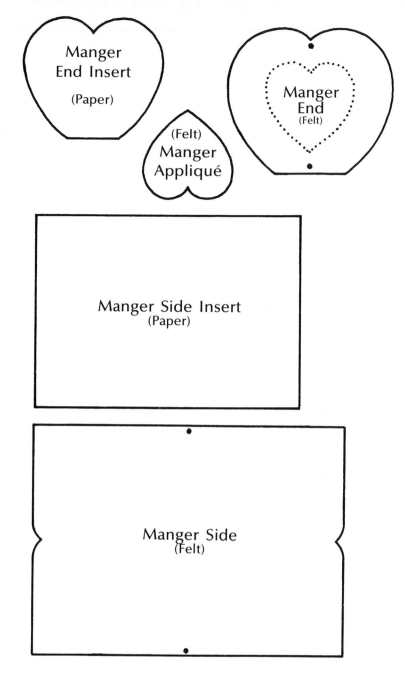

strands). Then attach one of the paper end inserts to the back of the piece, with a dot of craft glue. Add a plain felt end to cover the paper insert and baste around the outside edges. Repeat the process to complete the other end.

Use the placement dots and basting stitches to attach the manger ends to the side piece. Be sure to catch all four layers of felt. With a heart end facing you, blanket-stitch the pieces to join them together. When you reach the end of the side, continue stitching around the top of the heart. As you stitch, check to see if the stitches are even on both sides.

To flatten the bottom of the manger, pinch the felt side piece to fold the paper insert.

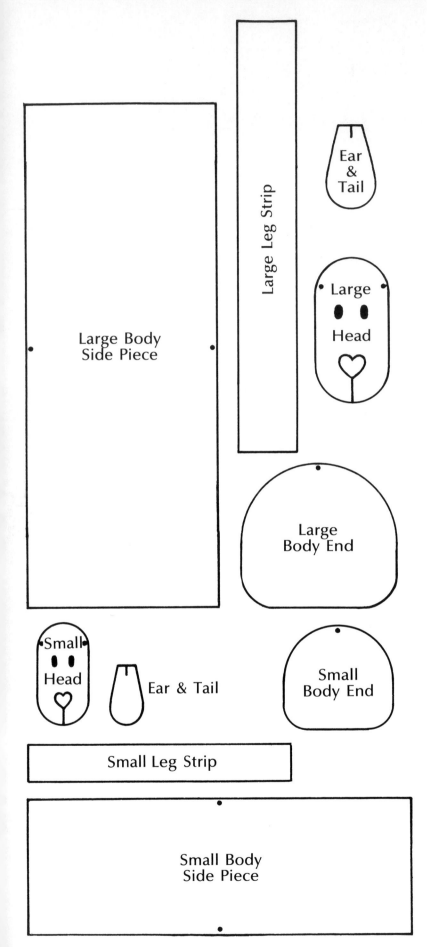

Ear & Tail

Large Leg Strip

Large Body Side Piece

Large Head

Large Body End

Small Head

Ear & Tail

Small Body End

Small Leg Strip

Small Body Side Piece

## SHEEP

**Materials** *(for one large, two small sheep)*
Cream felt, 8½" x 10"
Gray or taupe felt, 6½" x 8½"
Sewing thread: cream
Embroidery thread: 2 yards gray or taupe; 3½ yards cream; 18" each of brown, pink
Polyester stuffing

**1. Making the patterns**—Trace and label the patterns for each size sheep. Copy the matching dots. The pattern lines are the cutting lines for the felt. Make a template of each head pattern. Cut out the eyes and nose with a craft knife so you can easily transfer them to the felt. You may wish to embroider the face before cutting it out (see Step 5).

**2. Cutting the felt**—Select the desired size patterns and, on the wrong side of the cream felt, mark and cut out one body and two end pieces. From the dark felt, cut four legs, two heads, and three ear/tail pieces. Transfer the eyes and nose to one head. For the cream-colored sheep, cut all pieces from cream felt.

**3. Stitching the body**—Match the dot of the body to the dot at the top of one of the ends. Baste the body to the end, overlapping the edges at the center bottom. Blanket-stitch the basted edges, using cream embroidery thread (2 strands).

Baste the overlapped edges across the center bottom and stitch them together. Stuff the unit firmly. Baste the final end piece in place, matching the center top dot. Then blanket-stitch the edges.

**4. Forming the legs**—Fold back about ⅛" of the short end of one of the legs and stitch it in place. Using this edge as the starting point, roll up the strip tightly to create a cylinder. Attach the other end of the strip to the cylinder with blanket stitches. Add blanket stitches around the bottom of the cylinders. Repeat this procedure to make four legs for each sheep. Securely slipstitch each leg in place.

48

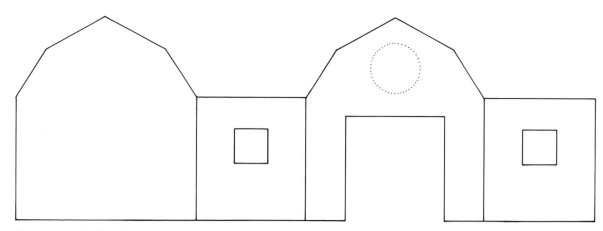

Figure 1: Making barn side pattern

**5. Making the head**—Using brown embroidery thread (1 strand), straight-stitch the eyes and nose line. Satin-stitch a pink heart nose. Pin the wrong sides of two heads together and join the edges with blanket stitches. Just before completing the stitches, add some stuffing. Edge all the single-layer ear and tail pieces with blanket stitches. Fold each piece in half lengthwise and tack the edges together at the top. Securely stitch an ear to each side of the head and use the remaining unit for a tail. Attach all pieces at the dots provided. Securely slipstitch the head to the body, extending it about ¼" above the back for the large sheep, and a little less for the small sheep.

## BARN
### Materials
Antique-red striped print, ⅜ yard
Green print, 7" x 9½"
Taupe fabric or felt, 7" x 9½"
Navy print, 16" x 16"
Cream felt, 3" x 5"
Beige felt, 3" x 3"
Putty-colored fabric, 13" x 30"
Thick polyester quilt batting, 24" x 40"
Heavy-weight interfacing, 24" x 40"
Sewing thread: antique-red, cream, navy
Embroidery thread: 18" beige, 1½ yards
   cream
Cream ¼" fold-over bias tape, 4 yards
Cream ½" fold-over bias tape, 3 yards
Flat cream crochet-type lace, ¼" to
   ⅜" wide, 1 yard
Two white Velcro fasteners, ½" diameter

**1. Making the patterns**—On folded paper trace the barn front with a cut-out door, and add the placement lines for the circular symbol. Use the same pattern for the back, but omit the door and the symbol placement line.

To make the complete pattern for the barn siding, trace two windowed side pieces and tape to the front and back, as shown in Figure 1. Copy a few dots to indicate the placement of bias tape.

Copy the patterns for the door/meadow, barn base/floor, and dotted placement lines for the bias tape. One edge of each of these pieces has a ¼" seam allowance included; other edges will be bound.

Draw the roof pattern on folded paper and transfer topstitching lines. Copy the heart and two circles for the felt symbol. Cut out the patterns and pierce the placement lines.

**2. Cutting the fabric**—Draw the complete barn siding pattern on the right side of a 13" x 30" piece of red fabric, but don't cut out the piece at this time. Copy the placement lines with a vanishing fabric marker.

From the remaining red fabric, cut one door and, with a vanishing fabric marker, mark the placement lines for the bias tape trim. Also cut out one red barn base. Pin the right sides of the door and base together and stitch where indicated on the pattern. Press the seam open.

Again use the door/meadow pattern to cut one meadow from the green print. Use the base/floor pattern to cut one barn floor from the taupe felt or fabric. Pin the pieces, right sides together, and stitch the seam. Press the seam open.

Mark and cut two navy pieces for the roof, transferring the topstitching lines on the front of one of them.

From the cream felt, cut four small hearts and one outer circle. From the beige felt, cut one inner circle.

From both the batting and the interfacing, cut the following pieces: 13" x 30" for the barn siding, 9" x 11¾" for the door/base, and 7" x 14⅜" for the roof.

**3. Preparing the barn siding**—Layer and pin together the materials as follows: putty fabric, right side down; interfacing; batting; red fabric with barn drawing, right side up.

Hand-baste around the inside of the barn and the outside of the windows, placing the stitches 3/16" from the edge, so that they will be placement lines for the bias tape. Don't cut out the piece yet. Machine-stitch around the inside of the barn and outside the window squares, stitching close to the outline (zigzag stitches are preferable). Now cut out the barn and the windows.

To make the symbol, baste or glue each heart in place on the inner circle. Then baste the inner circle to the outer circle. Blanket-stitch the hearts and the inner circle, using matching embroidery thread (2 strands). Baste the symbol in place on the front of the barn and blanket-stitch the edges.

**4. Binding the edges**—Mark and machine-stitch (straight stitches) the three vertical lines between the front, back, and side sections.

For placement of the bias tape, make a line of hand-basted stitches 3/16" from each side of the three vertical lines. Cut three lengths of the 1/4" bias tape, each 6¼" long. Open the center fold of one tape (but do not press it flat). Center the fold on one of the machine-stitched vertical lines that separate the barn sections. Hand-stitch each side of the tape. Add the remaining tapes in the same manner.

By hand, stitch the 1/4" bias tape to all the cut edges of the barn siding, making little tucks at the peaks of the roof sections and mitering the tape at the corners.

Binding the edges of the windows requires considerable patience. First, clip into each corner, making the cuts less than 1/8" deep. Cut a 9½" strip of the 1/4" bias tape and bind one of the square windows, mitering the tape at each corner. To create the effect of window panes, cut two 2½" strips of the 1/4" bias tape. Tuck under about 1/8" at each end and invisibly stitch the open edge closed. Center and tack the crossed strips to the bound edge

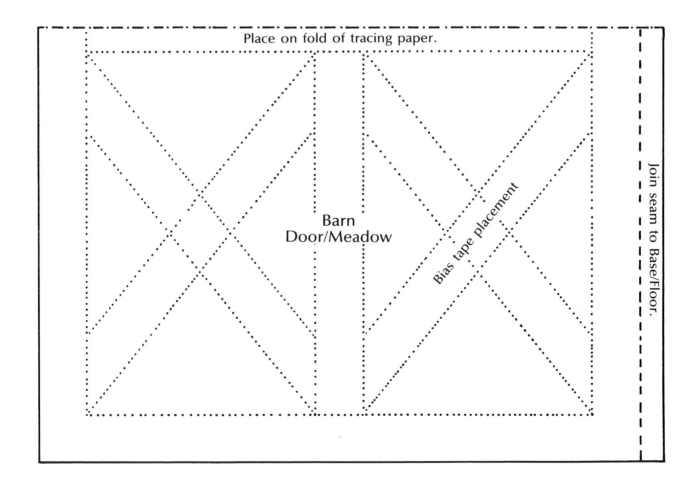

Place on fold of tracing paper.

Barn Door/Meadow

Bias tape placement

Join seam to Base/Floor.

of the window on the inside of the barn. Make the other square window.

Fold the barn siding into the barn shape, butting the two ends together and leaving the lining on the outside. Whipstitch the bias tape of the two butted edges together. Set the piece aside.

**5. Stitching the base and door**—Pin the barn base/door and floor/meadow pieces together in this order: red base/door, right side down; batting; interfacing; floor/meadow, right side up. The meadow should be directly over the door. Hand-baste the pieces together and also hand-stitch on top of the seam joining the sections. Then machine-stitch on the seam.

To make the flat bias trim for the door, cut a 64" strip of the ½" bias tape, open the center fold, and trim away about ¼" along the edge that has the widest fold. Refold the tape. Cut eight strips from this piece, each 4¾" long, to make the diagonal pieces. Baste and stitch each one in place on the door. Cut two 9" strips for the horizontal trim. Stitch

one across the center of the door and one at the bottom (one edge should touch the seam line). Cut and stitch a 6¼" vertical strip to the center of the door. Use the remaining untrimmed bias tape to bind the edges.

With the barn inside out, attach the base to the siding, using tiny whipstitches. Turn the barn right side out and invisibly stitch the front edges to the seam line between the floor and the meadow.

**6. Constructing the roof**—Layer and pin together the roof in this order: marked navy roof piece, right side up; unmarked navy roof piece, right side down; interfacing; batting. Machine-stitch around the edges, leaving about 2" open along one edge. Clip the corners and trim the batting. Turn right side out and invisibly close the opening. With seams precisely on the edges of the roof, baste around the outside edge. Machine-stitch along each peak and around the outside edge on the topstitching lines. Press the seamed edges and remove the basting stitches.

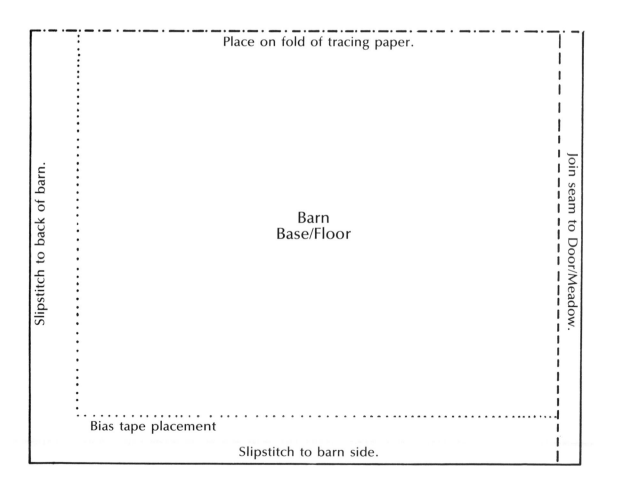

Place on fold of tracing paper.

Slipstitch to back of barn.

Join seam to Door/Meadow.

Barn
Base/Floor

Bias tape placement

Slipstitch to barn side.

**7. Adding the finishing touches—**Invisibly stitch the folded edge of the barn's top binding to the topstitching lines on the roof. On the front only, stitch the lace to the top of the barn just under the roof, either on or below the binding. Also add lace around the door opening.

Stitch the Velcro fasteners in place, one part of each unit to the binding on the front corner of the meadow, and the other part to the binding at each side of the barn front. Trim the units to fit.

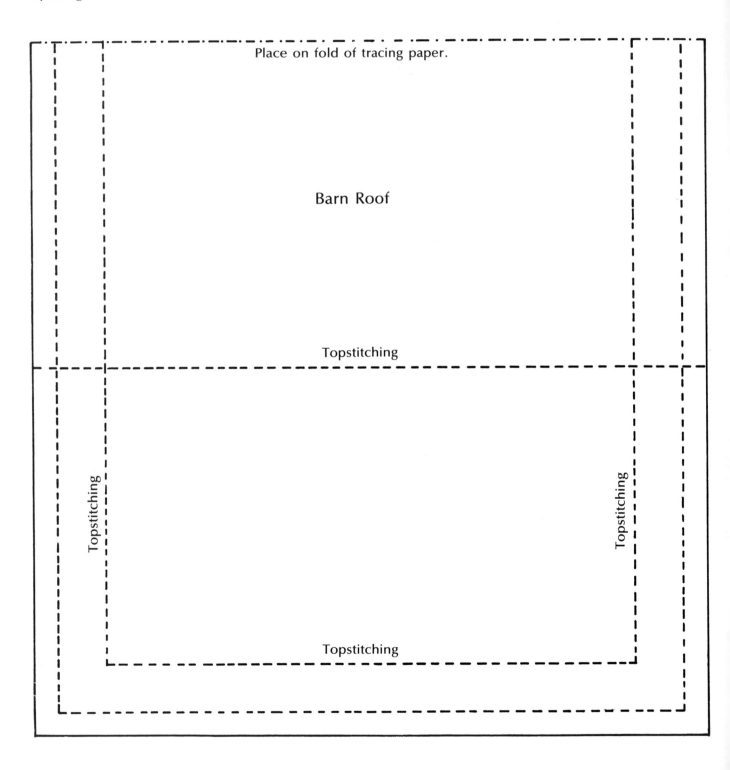

Place on fold of tracing paper.

Barn Roof

Topstitching

Topstitching

Topstitching

Topstitching

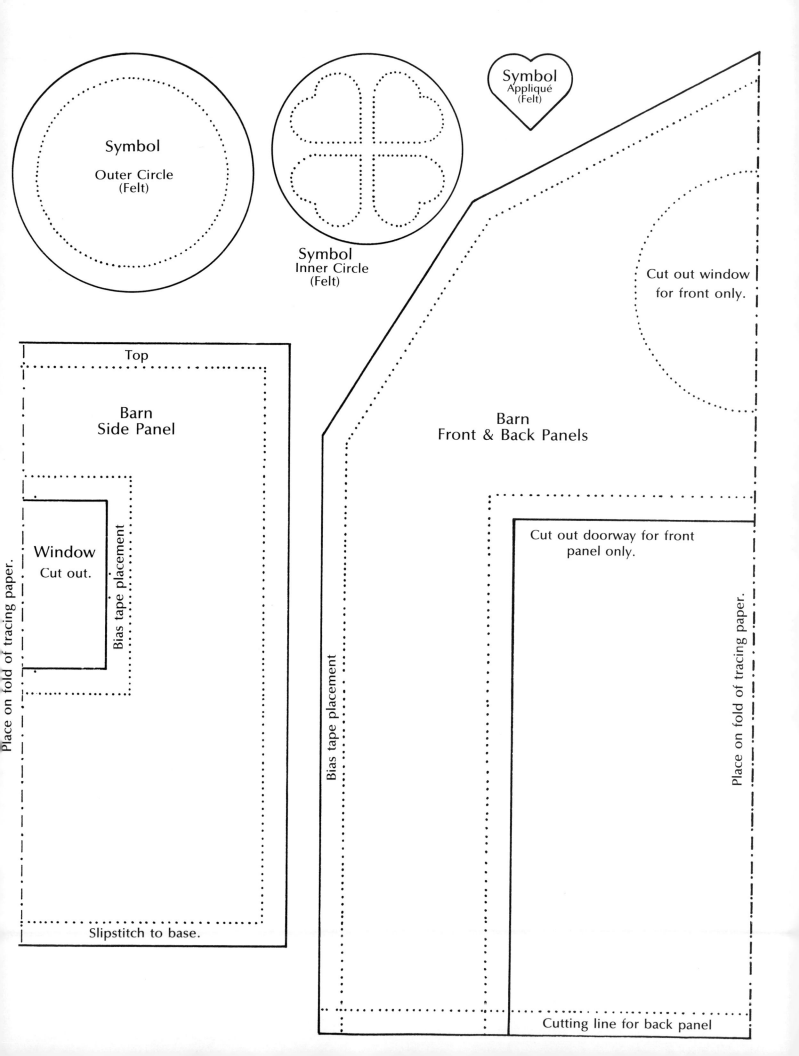

Symbol

Outer Circle
(Felt)

Symbol
Inner Circle
(Felt)

Symbol
Appliqué
(Felt)

Cut out window
for front only.

Top

Barn
Side Panel

Barn
Front & Back Panels

Window
Cut out.

Cut out doorway for front
panel only.

Bias tape placement

Bias tape placement

Place on fold of tracing paper.

Place on fold of tracing paper.

Slipstitch to base.

Cutting line for back panel

# WE WISH YOU A MERRY CHRISTMAS

Joyeux Noël! Feliz Navidad! Glad Jul! Fröhliche Weihnachten! There are many ways you can express your "Merry Christmas" wishes, and gift giving is certainly a language that everyone understands. When your presents are handmade, they speak an extra word of love.

This chapter offers a collection of heart-warming gifts for you to make. Each one is soft and lightweight, making it ideal to pack and send on its way with love.

# STAR PATCH PINCUSHION & TOTE

*The Star Patch motif, used for the wreath in Chapter 1, reappears here as a pincushion and a miniature tote bag. For a pretty yet practical gift, include colorful glass-topped pins and needles, folding scissors, and some small spools of thread. This is a great set to hang inside a closet or a kitchen cupboard to help quickly rescue drooping hemlines.*

**PINCUSHION**
**Materials**
Green-with-white dot scrap, 2¼" x 2¼"
Ecru scrap, 2¼" x 11½"
Green-and-red floral, 2¼" x 4¼"
Red scrap, 2¼" x 8"
Scrap for backing, 4½" x 4½"
Sewing thread: ecru, green
Polyester stuffing
Green ¼" fold-over bias tape, 22"
Green embroidery thread

**1. Making the patterns**—Trace, label, and copy the grain lines for the Star Patch patterns. The patterns are actual size and include ¼" seam allowances.
**2. Marking the fabrics**—Mark the grain lines on the back of the fabrics. Cut out the patches. Cut one green dot square and four ecru squares. Cut four floral triangles, eight red triangles, and four ecru triangles.

**3. Stitching the star patch**—Refer to Figure 1 and lay out the patches in order. Join the small triangles, right sides together, two at a time. Then stitch these larger triangles together to make four units. Stitch these units to the squares to make three horizontal rows, as shown in Figure 1. Join the three rows together to make a block. Press the seams open or toward the darkest fabric.

**4. Assembling the pincushion**—Pin the star patch to the backing fabric, wrong sides together, and machine-stitch around the outside, ¼" from the edges. Leave a 1½" opening for stuffing. Push stuffing into the corners, making the cushion plump, but flat. Close the opening and trim the seam allowance to ³/₁₆". Use invisible hand stitches to encase the edges in bias tape, starting at one corner and then mitering the tape as you go around each corner. When you return to the starting point, extend the tape to make a hanging loop. Close the open edge of the loop with invisible hand stitches, tucking under the cut end.

Trace the tiny heart pattern onto paper or acetate. Use a vanishing fabric marker to transfer it to each corner patch. Outline with green running stitches (1 strand).

### TINY TOTE
**Materials**
Red scrap, 2¼" x 2¼"
Ecru scrap, 4½" x 11"
Red-and-green floral, 2¼" x 4¼"
Green-with-white dot scrap, 2¼" x 8"
Scrap for lining, 4½" x 9"
Very thin quilt batting, 4¼" x 9"
Sewing thread: red, ecru, green
Red embroidery thread
Green ¼" fold-over bias tape, 28"

**1. Making the star patch**—Complete Steps 1–3 of the Pincushion, cutting one red square, four ecru squares, four floral triangles, eight green dot triangles, and four ecru triangles. Reserve a 4½" ecru square for the bag back.

**2. Assembling the tote**—Cut the lining scrap into two 4½" squares. Pin one square to the bag front and one to the bag back, placing the wrong sides together. Sandwich a thin layer of batting between layers.

Trace the small heart shape onto paper or acetate. Trace the heart pattern onto the ecru

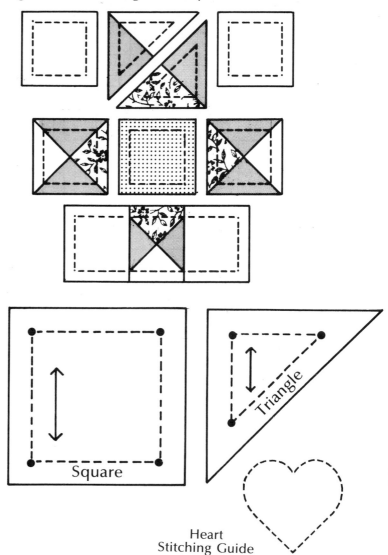

Figure 1: Assembling the star patch

Square

Triangle

Heart
Stitching Guide

squares with a vanishing fabric marker. Then outline the heart shapes with red running stitches (1 strand).

Machine-stitch around each square, ¼" from the edges. Trim one edge of each square to ³/₁₆" and encase that edge in a 4½" piece of bias tape. These edges will become the top opening of the bag. Pin the two squares together, lining sides touching and bound edges meeting. Machine-stitch ¼" from the unbound edges and then trim the seam allowances to ³/₁₆". Starting at the bottom of the bag, encase the edges in bias tape, extending the tape for the handle. Stitch the open edge of the handle closed.

# DUCK PLACE MATS

*This quicky and quacky place mat design is "duck soup" to make for a last-minute gift! "Ducks for Christmas?" you may be asking. Sure! A duck is one of those classic American folk-art motifs that look just right at any time of the year.*

*Any reversible print works well, but my favorite is the camouflage decoy. I wasn't able to find appropriate quilted fabric, so I quickly channel-quilted my own, and you can easily do that, too.*

**Materials** *(for two place mats and two napkins)*
Reversible print quilted fabric, ½ yard
Fold-over ¼" bias tape, 3¾ yards
Coordinating napkin-weight fabric, ½ yard
Sewing thread to match fabrics and binding
Two dark flat buttons, ⅜" to ½" diameter, or
   1 yard dark embroidery thread

**1. Preparing the fabric**—Secure the quilting stitches on the fabric by machine stitching along the cut edges. Preshrink the fabric by machine washing and partially drying it. If the fabric is then wrinkled, don't press it flat, but stretch the piece, secure it with pins, and hold a steam iron just above the surface.

**2. Making the pattern**—On a 17" x 22" piece of paper, draw a grid of 1¼" squares. Enlarge the duck place mat pattern, according to the directions in Supplies & Techniques. The pattern line is the cutting line. Mark the eye position and cut out the eye to make a template of the pattern.

**3. Marking and cutting the fabric**—Pin the duck pattern to the right side of the quilted fabric and, using a sharp soft pencil, trace around it and draw the eye. Before cutting the fabric, again secure the quilting threads, by machine stitching ⅛" inside the penciled outline. Make a second row of stitches 1/16" away from the first one, further inside the duck outline. This will provide a guideline for the bias tape.

   Cut out the duck on the pencil outline and lay it on a flat surface. If the edges pucker, clip the stitching threads and bobbin threads (not the fabric) at 2" or 3" intervals and gently pull to flatten. Diagonally clip ⅛" into the V area at the neck back.

**4. Adding the bias binding**—Bind the edge of the duck with bias tape, using the innermost stitching line as a placement guide. Invisibly hand-stitch the tape, first to one side and then to the other.

**5. Adding the eyes**—Stitch a button in position for the eye or use dark embroidery thread (2 strands) to satin-stitch a circle.

**6. Making the napkins**—Draw and cut an 18" square for each napkin and machine-baste ½" from the cut edges, to provide a guideline for the hem. Refer to Figure 1, and diagonally clip off ½" at each corner, to ease mitering. Press under the hem along the basting stitches. Fold under ¼" of the hem, fold under another ¼" to make a double hem, and then stitch by hand or machine. Remove the basting stitches.

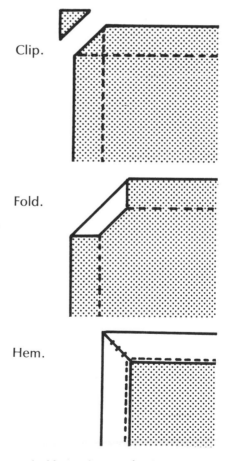

Clip.

Fold.

Hem.

Figure 1: Hemming and mitering the corners of the napkin

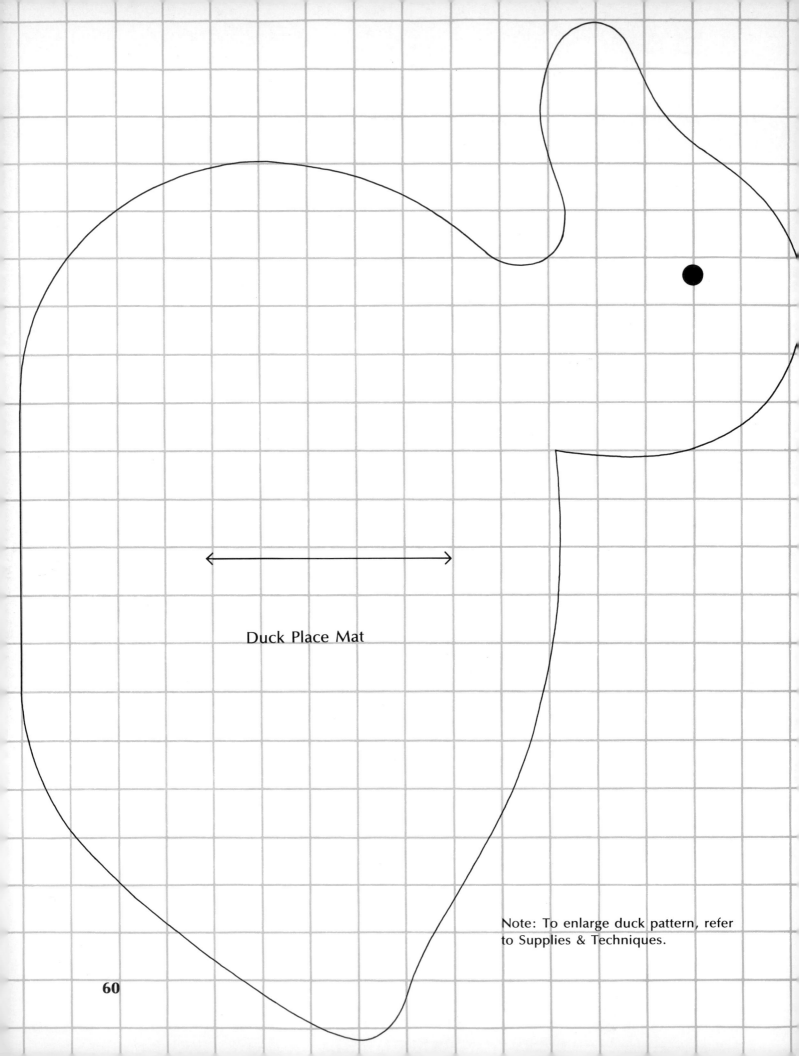

Duck Place Mat

Note: To enlarge duck pattern, refer to Supplies & Techniques.

# PUPPY LOVE PILLOW & QUILT

*How lovable Scottie dogs are, with their playful ways and "What's next?" expressions! Their squat little bodies and dark color make them such an appealing design motif.*

*The instructions for the Puppy Love Pillow are listed first, because you won't need more than a few scraps to make it. You'll definitely need more than just scraps for the quilt, however, even if you use a different fabric for each pup! If you purchase materials to make the quilt as it is shown, you'll have enough leftover pieces to make one matching pillow.*

# BUSY BASKET SEWING CADDY & PINCUSHION

*Basket quilts have been popular for a long time, to judge by the large collection of traditional basket blocks to be found in the old quilting books. The inspiration for this sewing caddy came from the Colonial Basket block. I wanted to add some flowers, so I selected one of the classic star motifs to stand in as daisies. The resulting design became a pocket and a pincushion for this portable sewing caddy—a Busy Basket!*

## SEWING CADDY
### Materials
Purple floral print fabric, ⅔ yard
Dark green-with-white dot fabric, ¼ yard
Thin quilt batting, 23" x 23"
Medium green scrap, 6" x 8"
Magenta scrap, 5" x 10"
Bright pink scrap, 5" x 5"
Light pink scrap, 3" x 5"
Dark green fold-over ¼" bias tape,
    2⅔ yards
Sewing thread: purple, dark green

**1. Making the patterns for the patchwork block**—Trace and label patterns A–F and their grain lines, but don't cut them out yet. Transfer the matching dots onto the D triangle. These patterns are all actual size and include ¼" seam allowances.

Paste the pattern tracings on lightweight cardboard or trace them directly onto thin flexible plastic, and cut them out. Pierce the dots on the D pattern, using a large needle.

**2. Making the remaining patterns and cutting the fabrics**—Dimensions are given for all the remaining pieces of the bag, so that they can be drawn directly on the proper fabrics and the batting. All the measurements include seam allowances.

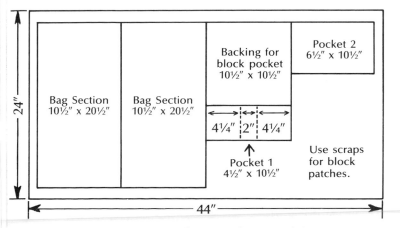

Figure 1: Layout for purple print fabric

Refer to Figure 1 and, on the back of the purple print fabric, mark and cut a 10½" square for the block backing and two 10½" x 20½" pieces for the bag sections. Also measure and cut a 4½" x 10½" piece for Pocket 1 and a 6½" x 10½" piece for Pocket 2. Lightly draw the topstitching lines, which will form small compartments on Pocket 1.

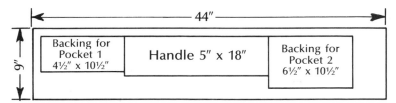

Figure 2: Layout for dark green dotted fabric

Refer to Figure 2 and, on the back of the dark green dotted fabric, mark and cut a 5" x 18" piece for the handle, a 4½" x 10½" piece for the Pocket 1 backing, and a 6½" x 10½" piece for the Pocket 2 backing.

From the batting, cut one 10½" x 20½" piece for the bag itself and one 10½" square for the patchwork block. Measure a 4½" x 10½" piece for Pocket 1 and a 6½" x 10½" piece for Pocket 2.

Set these pieces aside and reserve the remaining fabric scraps for the patchwork block.

**3. Marking the fabrics for the block patches**—Note the directions of the grain lines on the patterns and then, on the back of the purple print scraps, mark and cut out four A patches, four B patches, two C patches, two D patches, one E patch, and one F patch. Now flip the F pattern over and mark and cut out one F patch in reverse.

On the back of the dark green dotted fabric scraps, mark and cut out four B patches and twelve D patches, with their matching dots. Also measure and cut out six medium green D patches, with their matching dots.

On the back of the magenta scrap, draw sixteen B patches and cut them out. On the

# HERE COMES SANTA CLAUS

At Christmastime, what could be more fun than planning surprises for the children in your life? Sometimes just the thought of those bright little faces on Christmas morning is all the inspiration you need to start stitching. A glance through this chapter will give you lots of ideas for helping Santa fill up his sleigh with gifts of homemade happiness. Whether you stitch a new toy to hug or a quilt to cuddle, remember that you're also making a Christmas memory for your little one.

Would you like Santa Claus to make an early visit to your house this year? Stitch him up as a soft rag doll or a cozy bandanna pillow. Then make a few Holly Beary friends to sit on his lap. A great stocking stuffer, the Holly Beary is also the perfect little teddy to tuck into the hands of a sleeping child on Christmas Eve.

# MOUSE FAMILY IN A SWISS CHALET

*Mom and Dad and their seven little mousekins nestle together comfortably in their airy Swiss Chalet. You'll probably think of lots of ways to use the little mice. You could make very tiny felt cheese wedges, similar to the chalet but without the door. Pop in a mouse or two, and you have a Christmas ornament to hang on your tree. Making the seven thimble-size baby mice requires a light touch and a lot of patience. Remember, the first one is by far the hardest to make!*

*One warning—this toy is not suitable for a child under four years of age, because the baby mice are as tiny and as tempting as gumdrops. Play it safe and don't even give it to an older child if there are very young siblings at home.*

## Materials

Felt (preferably 50% wool), 8½" x 11" each: two gray, three creamy yellow
Gray sewing thread
Thin white cardboard, 8½" x 11"
Embroidery thread: 8 yards gray, 5 yards yellow, 2 yards pink, 2 yards black
Yellow ⅜" grosgrain ribbon, 9"
Yellow button, ¼" diameter
Polyester stuffing
Satin ribbons, each 9": ⅛" wide, two colors; ¹⁄₁₆" wide, seven colors

## CHEESE HOUSE

**1. Making the patterns**—Two pattern sets must be made for this project. Follow the outside lines to make one set for the felt pieces. Trace the inside lines around the toned area to make the patterns for the cardboard inserts.

Trace and label the patterns for the felt cheese front, back, and side panels, copying the holes. Trace the patterns for the cardboard inserts. To make the bases, trace a side panel, omitting the holes. No seam allowances are needed for the cheese. Cut out the patterns.

**2. Marking and cutting the pieces**—Using the patterns for the felt pieces, trace one front, one back, and the two sides on one piece of yellow felt. Place the marked felt piece on top of an unmarked one. Baste around every shape, ¹⁄₁₆" inside the lines, leaving one edge of each shape open. Don't baste around the holes yet.

Cut the remaining felt rectangle in half crosswise and, on one section, mark the base. Lay the marked felt on top of the unmarked felt piece. Baste around it, ¹⁄₁₆" inside the lines, leaving one edge open. Cut out all the pieces, but not the holes. Set the pieces aside.

Using the patterns for the cardboard pieces, mark one front, one back, one base, and the two sides on the white cardboard. Cut out each insert, reserving the cardboard scraps for the bases of the mice. Use a craft knife to cut out each hole, and please be careful!

**3. Preparing the units**—Push each insert into its corresponding felt pocket. Hold the units against the light to be sure the hole positions align. Baste each opening closed, stitching about ¹⁄₁₆" from the edge. Also baste around

each hole, making the stitches about ¹⁄₁₆" outside of each circle. Cut out each felt hole, using the craft knife or embroidery scissors.

Edge each hole with blanket stitches, using yellow embroidery thread (2 strands).

**4. Assembling the units**—Baste the front and the back to the base, ¹⁄₁₆" from the cut edges. When you do this, a narrow ridge, almost like a seam allowance, will form on the outside of the cheese. Blanket-stitch the edges together along the ridges. Set this section aside.

To make the handle, stitch the ends of the yellow grosgrain ribbon together and then baste the ends to the inside of one of the side units between the dots. Baste and blanket-stitch the two side units together along the top peaked edge, catching the ribbon in your stitches. Baste the sides to the base and to the back.

Finish all the edges of the house with blanket stitches, making extra stitches at the corners for security. Stitch the button to the apex of the front door and make a buttonhole loop at the front peak of the roof, using the embroidery thread.

## LARGE MICE

**1. Making the patterns**—Trace the patterns. The solid pattern lines indicate cutting lines for the felt. The broken pattern lines indicate machine-stitching lines. Copy the features and the dots onto the patterns, and pierce them with a large needle.

**2. Cutting and stitching the felt**—Cut one piece of gray felt into four 3" x 5" rectangles. On one, draw the mouse body and two arms, leaving ¼" between the pieces. Pin this piece, right side up, to one of the unmarked rectangles. Using the tiniest stitch setting and backstitching at the beginning and end of each seam, machine-stitch the body and each arm. Do not stitch the edges marked "open" along the bottom. Cut out the pieces, leaving seam allowances about ¹⁄₁₆" wide around the stitching lines. Cut precisely on the outline of each edge marked "open." Use the scraps to cut out two ears and one base.

Use the two remaining 3" x 5" rectangles of gray felt and repeat the process, to make the pieces for another large mouse. In addition, cut a cardboard base for both of the large mice.

**3. Stuffing and completing the body**—Turn each body right side out. Hold the pattern against each side of the felt unit and use a vanishing fabric marker to transfer the features and ear-placement dots. After the head is stuffed, it will change shape, so you may decide to change the placement of the ears and features. The markings will disappear with time.

Stuff the head portion very firmly, using a crochet hook or the blunt end of a pencil, and mold its shape as you stuff it. Push lots of stuffing into the body area, too, so that it will be very firm. Press the cardboard base against the opening, fitting it snugly within the felt edges and matching the dots with the front and back seams. Place the felt base on top of the cardboard, matching the dots with the seams again, and baste it to the mouse. Use gray embroidery thread (2 strands) to blanket-stitch the base. Remove the basting stitches.

Wrap gray embroidery thread (2 strands) very tightly around the neck of the mouse, to define the head. Knot the threads and trim the ends. To a degree, you can mold the head so that it will be elongated or short.

**4. Attaching the ears**—Fold an ear in half and make a little knotted stitch along one edge, ⅛″ from the fold, to hold it in a creased position. Pin each ear to the head, to judge its position, and then stitch it in place as invisibly as possible. It seems easiest to do this by passing the needle through the head, from one ear to the other. Catch only the area that you originally stitched at the fold or the inside crease of each ear.

**5. Adding the features**—Determine the correct position for the features and use black

embroidery thread (2 strands) to satin-stitch the eyes. Straight-stitch the nose, nose line, and mouth, using pink thread (2 strands).

**6. Braiding the tail**—Cut three 12″ lengths of gray embroidery thread (6 strands). Thread a large-eyed needle and pass the needle through the base at the center-back seam, pulling the thread halfway through, so that you have two 6″ ends. Repeat the process with the other two thread lengths, so that you have six thread ends. Pin the mouse to your work surface. Tightly braid the six pieces together into a 3″ length and knot the ends together. Trim away any thread ends.

**7. Creating the arms**—It will be difficult to turn the arms right side out without stretching the cut edge. Use the following technique to make the task easier. Thread a needle with a doubled and knotted thread. Push the needle into one of the paws, pass it through the inside space, and then pull the thread, to help turn the arm right side out. Remove the thread, and push a little stuffing into each paw.

Close the arm openings with blanket stitches and then attach them to the body as invisibly as possible, about ⅛″ down from the neck and about ½″ from the center front seam. Tie a bow around the neck of each mouse, using the ⅛″-wide ribbon.

**SMALL MICE**
**1. Making the mouse**—Cut a gray piece of felt into fourteen 2¼″ x 2½″ rectangles and complete Steps 1–5 for the Large Mice. Disregard all references to arms, since the small mice have none. Use one strand of embroidery thread to attach the base and stitch the features. Tie a bow around the neck, using the ¹⁄₁₆″-wide ribbon.

**2. Braiding the tail**—Cut three 5″ lengths of gray embroidery thread. Thread a large-eyed needle with one of the lengths (6 strands). Pass the needle and thread under the felt base and exit at the center back, leaving about ½″ under the base and 4½″ extending beyond the mouse. Repeat the procedure with all three lengths of thread, and then stitch the threads securely to the base at the center back. Pin the mouse to your work surface. Tightly braid the pieces together, forming a 1⅜″ length. Knot and trim the ends.

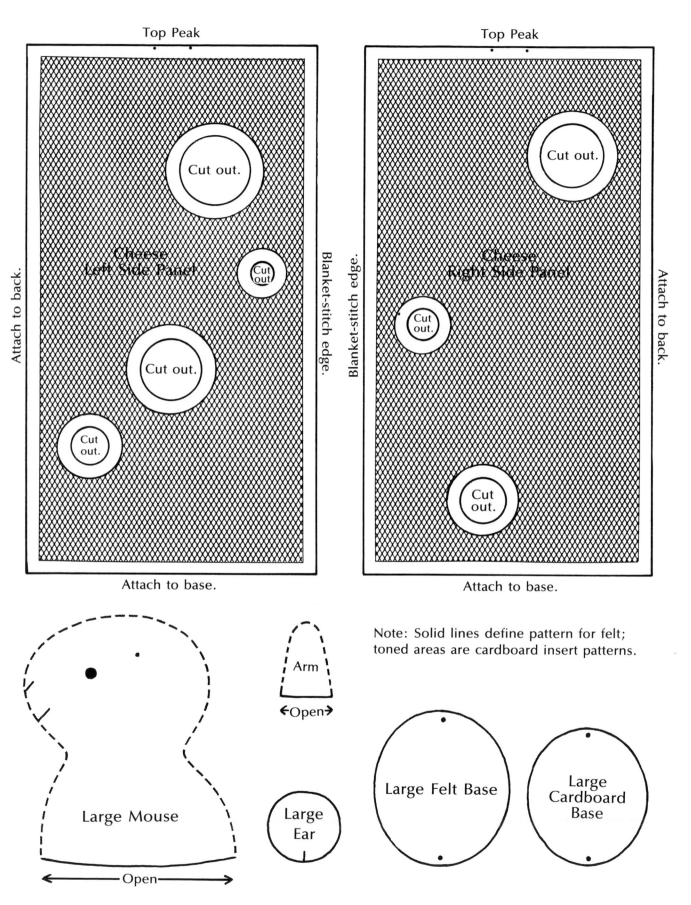

Top Peak

Cut out.

Cut out

Cut out.

Cut out.

Attach to back.

Cheese
Left Side Panel

Blanket-stitch edge.

Attach to base.

Top Peak

Cut out.

Cut out.

Cut out.

Cheese
Right Side Panel

Blanket-stitch edge.

Attach to back.

Attach to base.

Arm

←Open→

Note: Solid lines define pattern for felt;
toned areas are cardboard insert patterns.

Large Mouse

←——Open——→

Large
Ear

Large Felt Base

Large
Cardboard
Base

**91**

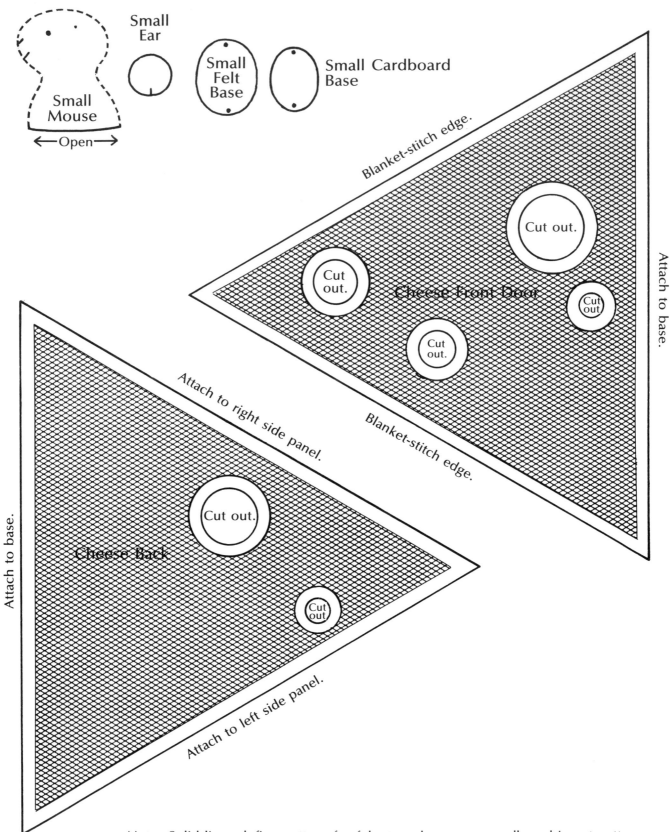

Small
Ear

Small
Felt
Base

Small Cardboard
Base

Small
Mouse

←Open→

Blanket-stitch edge.

Cut out.

Cut
out.

Cheese Front Door

Cut
out.

Cut
out.

Attach to base.

Attach to right side panel.

Blanket-stitch edge.

Cut out.

Cheese Back

Cut
out.

Attach to base.

Attach to left side panel.

Note: Solid lines define pattern for felt; toned areas are cardboard insert patterns.

# SANTA BIB

*Santa's sweet pudgy face adorns this simple-to-stitch bib for baby's first Christmas, or even second! Mini-dot fabric suggests a snow flurry, and all the appliqués are quilted to make the bib very soft and puffy. A cute touch would be to substitute thin white terry cloth for the white piqué that I used for the beard, so Santa could be soft and fuzzy, too.*

**Materials**
Blue-with-white pin-dot scrap, 8" x 11"
Red-with-white pin-dot scrap, 3" x 6"
Opaque white scrap, 8" x 8"
Pink scrap, 4" x 4½"
Thin quilt batting, 8" x 11"
Contrasting scrap for backing, 8" x 11"
Sewing thread: white, red, pink
Embroidery thread: 1 yard pink; ½ yard
   each, white, blue, red
White fold-over ¼" bias tape, 2¼ yards
Purchased white snowflake, 1" diameter

**1. Making the patterns**—Trace the bib, hat, and face from the book. On folded tracing paper, draw the beard/hatband pattern. Copy all dots, embroidery details, and placement lines on all the pieces. Pierce the placement lines and dots with a large needle. Cut out the eyes, nose, and cheeks, and cut along the mouth line to make a template of the face pattern. All the pattern lines are cutting lines for this project.

**2. Marking and cutting the fabrics**—From the blue dot fabric, cut one bib and mark the hat and beard placement lines. Use the red dot scrap to cut out one hat. Also cut one white beard/hatband piece, marking the face placement lines. If the fabric is not opaque enough, back it with another layer of white fabric. Cut out a pink face, lightly marking the features on the right side of the fabric.

**3. Preparing the hat and beard**—Mark the ¼" seam allowances around the hat and clip the curves at the top and side. Fold the seam allowances of the top and side edges to the back. Invisibly appliqué the hat to the bib front.

Mark the ¼" seam allowances around the beard. Cut a 14" length of the bias tape and bind only the top of the beard/hatband piece from dot to dot. Make a little pleat at each indentation of the scallops. Invisibly hand-stitch the binding to one side of the beard, and then to the other. Taper the binding to the dots, pushing the excess to the back of the beard and stitching it there. Appliqué the

bound edge to the bib, overlapping the lower edge of the hat and matching the scalloped edges.

**4. Creating the face**—Mark the ¼" seam allowance around the face with basting stitches. Clip around the curve; fold the seam allowance to the back. Invisibly hand-stitch the face to the beard.

Satin-stitch (2 strands) blue eyes, a red nose, white eyebrows, and pink cheeks. The mouth will be stitched in the final step.

**5. Assembling the bib**—On a flat work surface, spread the backing fabric, right side down. Top it with the layer of batting and then add the bib front, right side up. Pin and baste the layers together, ¼" from the edges. Trim the batting and backing layers to match the bib shape.

Machine-stitch around the bib, ⅛″ from the edges. Invisibly hand-stitch the bias tape around the outside edge, leaving the neck unbound.

Cut a 30″ length of tape, center it on the neck edge, and invisibly stitch it in place. Leave a 12″ tie at each end. Tuck under ¼″ at each cut end, and invisibly stitch along the open edges of the ties.

**6. Adding the finishing touches**—Quilt around the hat, the hatband, and the face. Pass the needle from the front through to the back of the fabric, to make everything very puffy. Backstitch (1 strand) the mouth red, making the stitches go through to the back of the bib. This will make the face rather pudgy. To create a tassel on the hat, securely tack on a lace snowflake.

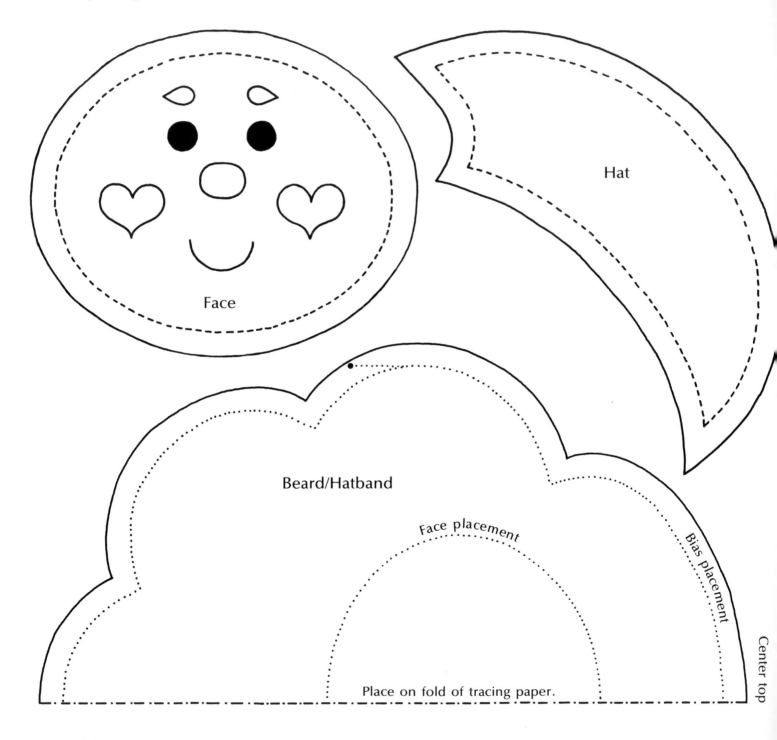

Face

Hat

Beard/Hatband

Face placement

Bias placement

Place on fold of tracing paper.

Center top

94

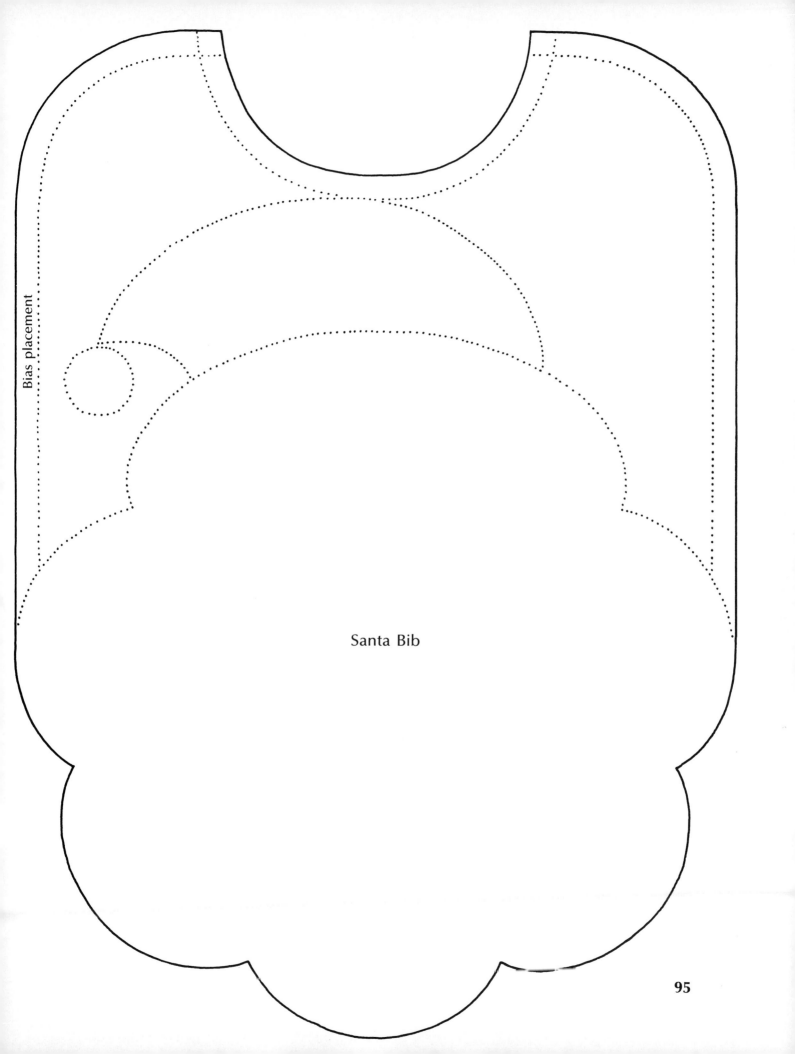

Bias placement

Santa Bib

95

# SANTA DOLLS

*Santa is such a softy, when you stitch him as a cuddly Christmas companion! You can make a 16-inch doll that's just the right size to hug, or you can use the grid to enlarge the patterns and create a 32-inch Santa pillow that seems big enough to hug you right back!*

*Stitching the little doll is really a snap! The results are especially cute when you empty out your scrap bag and mix patterns and prints. For a more elegant Santa, use scraps of rich velveteen and pieces of pretty lace.*

## SANTA PILLOW
### Materials
Four matching red bandanna handkerchiefs, each approximately 22" square
Green print or solid scrap, 12" x 12"
Black scrap, 18" x 23"
White felt, two pieces, each 8½" x 11"
Light pink scrap, 4½" x 11½"
Medium pink scrap, 2" x 4"
Sewing thread: red, black, medium pink
Embroidery thread: 2½ yards white, 18" black
Polyester stuffing
Red pom-pom, ¾" diameter (optional)
White pom-pom, 1½" diameter (optional)

**1. Making the patterns**—Draw a grid of 1" squares and enlarge all of the pillow patterns, according to the directions in Supplies & Techniques. When you enlarge the patterns, ½" seam allowances will automatically be included where they are necessary.

In order to use the bandanna borders effectively, do not place the upper coat and lower coat patterns on fold as the patterns specify. In place of the fold, use a seam. Draw the patterns for the upper coat and the lower coat, adding a ½" seam allowance to each edge labeled "Place on fold of fabric."

Make a template of the head pattern by cutting out the eyes, nose, and cheek. You will use the cheek cutout as a pattern later.

**2. Marking and cutting the fabrics**—As you work, trace the borders and other motifs on the patterns, so that you can match them on all the fabric pieces that you cut. Refer to Figure 1 and place the lower coat pattern on the corner of one bandanna. The printed corner of the border (represented by the gray area) should rest inside the coat area, not within the seam allowance. Mark and cut out the piece. Then flip the pattern over, and cut one lower coat in reverse. Mark and cut out one upper coat and one in reverse. These

border pieces will be used for the front of the Santa. Also cut one hat.

Using a second bandanna and referring to Figure 2, mark and cut another lower coat and one in reverse. Since these are for Santa's back, use the border, but not the corners. Also cut out one sleeve, one reverse sleeve, and another hat.

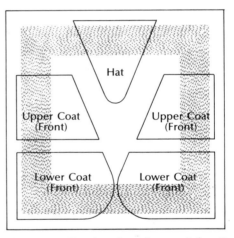

Figure 1: Cutting bandanna 1 for Santa Pillow

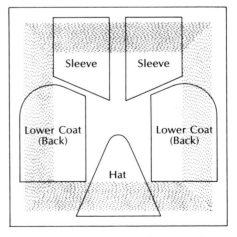

Figure 2: Cutting bandanna 2 for Santa Pillow

# FLANNEL TEDDY COMFORTER

*This soft-as-a-cloud Teddy Comforter is especially easy and nice for baby's long winter naps. But if you are thinking of making it for a summer baby, suggest that it be used as a precious pastel wall hanging until cool weather comes. Baste four or five ribbon loops along the top edge and slip them over a dowel or a cafe curtain rod.*

*This comforter is easy to stitch, because almost the entire quilt is made using just square and triangle patches. Only the eyes, nose, cheeks, and vest buttons are appliquéd, and the layers are tied together instead of quilted.*

**Materials** *(for 41" x 48" quilt)*
Pale yellow flannel, 3 yards
Pale pink flannel, ¼ yard
Pale blue flannel, ½ yard
Pale green flannel, ½ yard
White flannel, ⅛ yard
Crib-size quilt batting, extra-loft or ultra-loft
    (or a remnant, at least 44" x 55")
Sewing thread: pink, blue, white
White ½" fold-over bias tape, 6 yards
Embroidery thread: 2 yards pale blue,
    10 yards white

**1. Preparing the fabric**—If you work with 100% cotton flannel, it would be a good idea to gently prewash your fabrics in cold water and machine-dry them at a low setting. To keep the edges from unraveling during the prewash, pink each cut end. If you're giving the comforter as a gift, be sure to include a note that contains laundering advice: cold-water washing and low-temperature drying.

**2. Making the patterns**—Since you will be cutting many patches, it's best to make master patterns, using a clear or frosted flexible plastic. Trace the patterns onto the plastic, directly from the book. Cut out, using a craft knife. With a pencil, draw around the master patterns on the backs of fabrics.

As an alternative to patterns, you can draw the squares and triangles directly on the fabrics, as I did. Tape the fabric to a flat surface and measure and mark as many squares and triangles as required.

**3. Cutting the patches**—All the measurements and patterns include ¼" seam allowances. Refer to Figure 1 and, on the back of the yellow flannel, measure and cut two border pieces, each 5½" x 42", and two more border pieces, each 5½" x 44". Borders are cut extra long and backing is cut extra large to allow for variations in size of the comforter top.

From the yellow flannel, cut one hundred

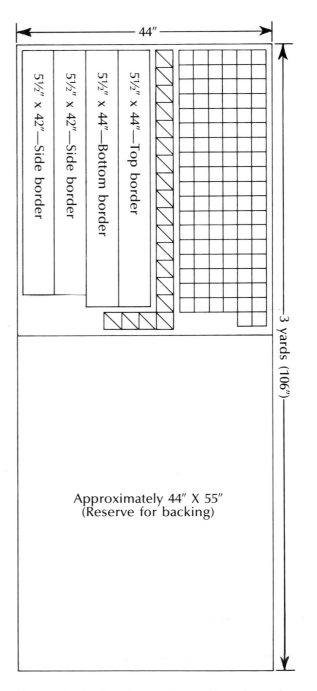

Figure 1: Cutting layout for yellow flannel

# PIGGY PATCH PROJECTS

Here's a Piggy Patch design that might set you off on a number of needlework projects. Patterns are provided for a quilted tote and a tiny piggy bank purse for your favorite little girl. But you could use the same patterns and create a cuddly pillow top, a toy, or even a pot holder for your kitchen.

## PIGGY PATCH TOTE
### Materials
White opaque scrap, 17" x 35"
White-with-green dot fabric, 19" x 31"
Pink-with-white floral scrap, 8" x 15"
Blue-with-white floral scrap, 10" x 20"
Two scraps of green-with-white floral
   (different prints), each 5" x 10"
Thin polyester quilt batting, 19" x 31"
White sewing thread
Blue button, ¼"–⅜" diameter
Blue embroidery thread, 18"
Green ¼" fold-over bias tape, 3⅞ yards
White ¼" fold-over bias tape, 4½" (or white
   ¼" grosgrain ribbon, 4½")

**1. Making the patterns**—I prefer to measure and draw patches directly on the fabrics, without using any patterns. Tape the fabric to a flat surface and measure and mark as many 1½" squares as required. To make triangles, draw 1⅞" squares and then divide each square diagonally.

However, since I know some people prefer full-size patterns, they are given here as well. If you use the patterns, make a plastic master pattern from clear or frosted vinyl. Trace the patterns directly from the book onto the plastic, marking the seam allowances. Trace around the patterns onto the fabric, as many times as needed.

Choose one method or the other (don't use a combination), because patches drawn with master patterns will be slightly larger than those measured and drawn on the fabrics.

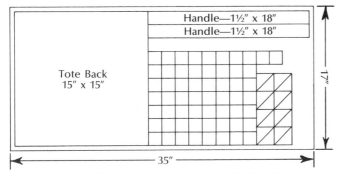

Figure 1: Cutting layout for white fabric

**2. Cutting the fabrics**—Refer to Figure 1 for the suggested cutting layout of the white fabric. Cut a 15" square for the tote back, two 1½" x 18" strips for handles, and 58 squares and 15 triangles.

From the white-with-green dot, cut two 1½" x 18" strips for the handles and two 15" squares for the front and back linings.

From the pink floral, cut 37 squares and 11 triangles. From the blue floral, cut 51 squares and 10 triangles. From the green floral, cut 15 squares from each of the two different prints and two triangles from each of the two different prints. From the batting, cut two 15" squares and two 1½" x 18" handles.

**3. Arranging the patches**—On a portable flat surface, lay out the patches in separate rows, referring to the photograph and Figure 2 for placement.

Figure 2: Completed tote front

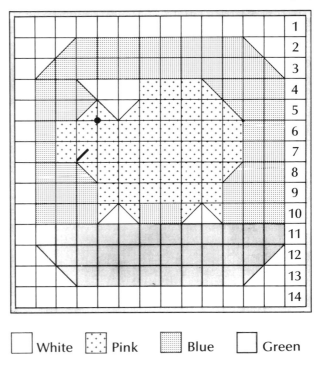

Rows

☐ White   ☐ Pink   ▦ Blue   ☐ Green

**4. Stitching the patches**—Stitch the triangle patches together to form squares, before you sew the squares together to form rows. Check Figure 2 for color placement. Press the seams open or toward the darkest patches.

**5. Making the rows**—Start at the top left corner and stitch the patches together to form separate rows. There is no need to pin individual patches together. When joining triangle and square patches, always match up a 90° corner. Press the seams open or toward the darkest fabric.

# SOCK BABIES

*These tiny sock dolls are baby-soft, baby-cute, and baby-safe, because all of the clothes and trimmings are stitched on securely. Sock dolls have been made for a long, long time—they're part of our folk-art tradition. Each of these little ones is cut and stitched from a single nylon toddler sock. A second contrasting sock provides the material for a pair of booties and a diaper. Then scraps of fabric, ribbon, and lace are fashioned into baby dresses, sacques, or shirts.*

### BASIC SOCK BABY
**Materials**

One pink, tan, or brown stretch-nylon toddler sock for body, size 4 to 5½ (see Figure 1)

White or colored stretch-nylon toddler sock for diaper and booties, size 4 to 5½ (see Figure 5)

Sewing thread to match

Polyester stuffing

Embroidery thread: 18″ blue, brown, or black; 1½ yards hair color; 16″ white

Powdered blusher, optional

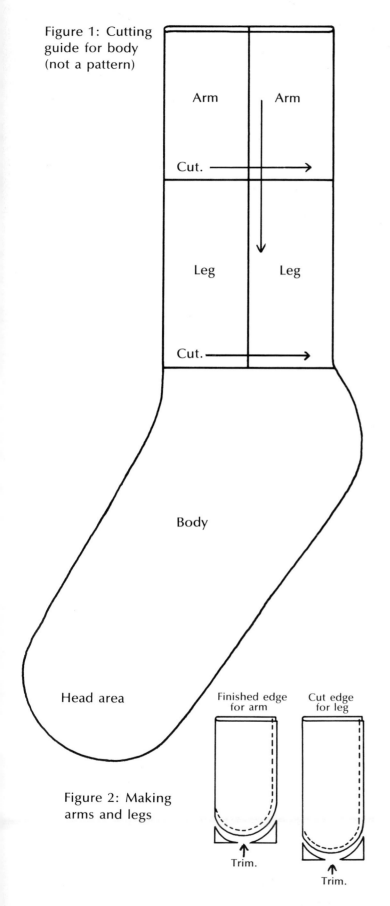

Figure 1: Cutting guide for body (not a pattern)

Arm    Arm

Cut. ———→

Leg    Leg

Cut. ———→

Body

Head area

Finished edge for arm

Cut edge for leg

Trim.

Trim.

Figure 2: Making arms and legs

**1. Cutting the sock**—Refer to Figure 1 and compare the size of your sock to the drawing. Hand-wash (make that scrub) any printed labels. Be sure to dry the sock naturally, so that it won't shrink. Stretch the sock a bit to adjust the size, if necessary. Figure 1 is a guide, not a pattern, since sock sizes vary.

Use a vanishing fabric marker to draw the interior solid lines suggested in Figure 1. Use super-sharp scissors to cut the sock in half, cutting along the heel line. The foot of the sock will be used to form the head and body of the baby (the heel will be its little bottom). To make the baby's arms and legs, cut the leg of the sock into four sections. Don't cut along the folded edges. All of the pieces will appear to be too short, but they'll lengthen as they're stuffed.

**2. Stitching the body**—To make the baby's head, start stuffing the toe area of the sock. Stuff the entire body, until it's pudgy and fairly firm. Use your hands to mold and sculpt the body as you stuff, and try to push the toe seam towards the top of the head area. The front of the sock will be the front of the doll. Turn under the cut edge of the heel and pull it over the opening, overlapping the sock front. Neatly sew the opening closed. At this point, the body should be about 4½" long and 6½" around.

To form the head, use a doubled thread, matching the color of the sock, and take a stitch about midway, at the center back of the doll. Knot the stitch, leaving a 3" length of doubled thread. Wrap the thread around the stuffed sock several times, pulling the thread enough to define the head. Take another stitch and tie all the thread ends together. Gently mold the doll, to make a cute rounded head and a slightly elongated body.

**3. Making the arms and legs**—To make an arm, take one of the appropriate pieces of the sock and fold the right side to the inside. Use a vanishing fabric marker to draw the seam line, and then hand-stitch, as indicated in Figure 2, making sure that the finished edge of the sock is at the top of the arm. The seam should be about ¹⁄₁₆" wide and your stitches very tiny, but not too tight. Trim the corners around the curve. Turn the arm right side out and stuff it, stretching it to about 2". Use overcasting stitches to close the top opening without turning under the edge.

The leg is made just as the arm is, but the top edge is cut instead of finished. To avoid runs along this cut edge, be especially careful when you turn the leg right side out, stuff it, and stitch it closed. Don't bother to turn under the cut edge at the top, because it will be covered by a diaper later. Flatten and stretch the leg to about 2¾". Make two arms and two legs for the baby.

**4. Attaching the arms and legs**—Refer to Figure 3 for placement of the legs. Stitch the legs to the seam on the bottom of the body, with the seams of the legs on the inside. To suggest little feet, fold the bottom of each leg forward and tack it, making the stitches as neat and tiny as possible, even though the feet may later be covered with booties.

Experiment to find the best position for the arms. I stitched them about ⅛" below the neck, and turned them so that the side seams were under the arms as shown in Figure 3. Use doubled thread to define the hands, as you did the head in Step 2, making them about ½" long. Stitch four short parallel lines on each hand, to indicate fingers.

**5. Marking the face**—The circumference of the doll's head should be about 6½". Trace the face guide from Figure 4 on a 2" square of paper and pierce the dotted lines with a large needle. Flatten the doll's head a bit, and center the guide on the face so that the B points are about ⅝" up from the neck. Tape the guide in place and use a vanishing fabric marker to transfer the dots.

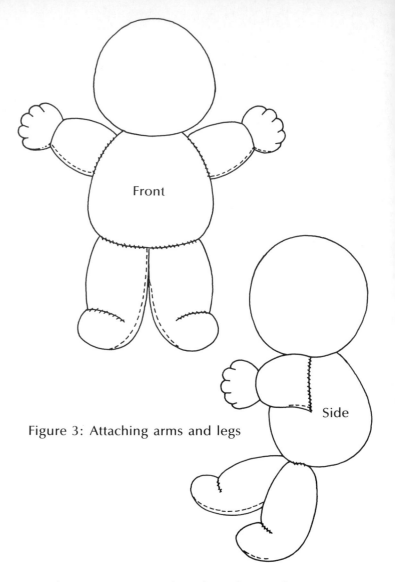

Figure 3: Attaching arms and legs

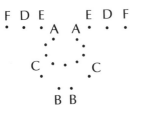

Figure 4: Face guide

**6. Stitching the face**—Before you stitch the face on the finished doll, experiment with the technique. It may seem confusing at first, but you'll soon master the procedure, if you read through the instructions and refer to the face guide. Each face will look just a little different—sort of laughable and lovable!

Thread a small needle with a 25" length of strong, unknotted sewing thread to match the sock color. To form the nose, insert the needle at one A dot, and use the tiniest of

stitches to sew around to the other A dot. Leave 12" tails of thread extending at each side. There should be no stitches across the bridge of the nose. Add another needle to the thread end that is free. Stitching the face with the two needles helps to make the features symmetrical.

Re-insert each needle at the nearest A dot and exit at the A dot on the opposite side. The thread will be on the inside of the head, so it won't show on the bridge of the nose. Pull each thread end to form the nose. Use a pin to pull stuffing into the nose, but try to avoid snagging the sock. Take a tiny stitch and knot each thread at each A dot, but don't trim the threads.

On each side of the face, insert the needles again at the nearest A dot and exit at the B dot below it, passing the thread through the inside of the head. As you pull out the threads, pinch the nose and the mouth together to form the upper lip. Remove the

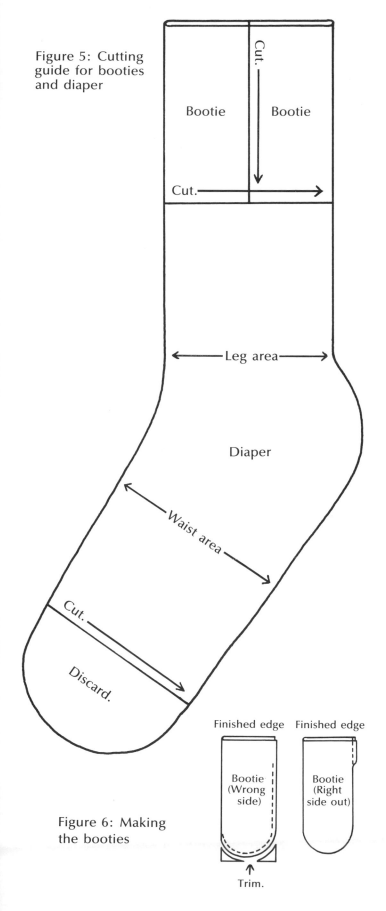

Figure 5: Cutting guide for booties and diaper

Cut.

Bootie | Bootie

Cut.

Leg area

Diaper

Waist area

Cut.

Discard.

Finished edge | Finished edge

Bootie (Wrong side) | Bootie (Right side out)

Trim.

Figure 6: Making the booties

needles and tie the threads together between the two B dots.

Thread the needles again and insert each one at the nearest point B, exiting at the C dot just above it. Take a tiny stitch on the spot, and then knot each thread at each point C. Again insert each needle at each C dot and exit at the D spot above it, pinching C and D together to make the cheek. Pull the thread tightly and knot it at the D spot.

To make the eye lines, stitch from D to E, leaving the thread on the outside of the head. After inserting the needle at E, exit at F, pulling the thread and knotting it at F. Leaving the thread on the outside, insert the needle again at D and exit at E. Make a stitch across each eyelid and knot each thread.

Make large, colored French knots (3 strands) for eyes, or stitch straight across the eyelid with hair-colored thread (2 strands) to make a sleepy baby. If you wish, use a fine paintbrush or Q-tip to apply a little powdered blusher to the cheeks.

**7. Adding the hair**—Securely stitch a few loops of embroidery thread (3 strands at a time) to the front of the head. Add a cap or bonnet, and trim the loops to make soft fringe or leave them to suggest curls.

**8. Making the booties**—Refer to Figure 5 and cut off a portion of the sock cuff, reserving the remaining piece for the diaper. Cut the cuff in half lengthwise. Fold each rectangle in half lengthwise, placing the right side inside and the finished edge along the top. Hand-stitch a ¹⁄₁₆" seam as in Figure 6, starting the seam about ³⁄₈" below the finished top edge. Turn the bootie right side out and complete the unstitched seam on the outside. Put the bootie on the doll's foot and fold down the cuff. Invisibly stitch the booties to the legs. To make the tie, cut an 8" length of the six-strand embroidery thread and knot each end. Tie the thread around the leg below the cuff and make a bow.

**9. Making the diaper**—Again referring to Figure 5, trim the remaining portion of the sock, to use as a diaper. Pull the resulting tube over the doll's body, positioning the heel on the baby's bottom. Tuck under the cut edges to make a doubled diaper, taking special care to prevent runs. Invisibly stitch the diaper to the doll around the waist and the legs, covering the rough edges around the leg tops.

**113**

## SHORT DRESS
### Materials
Fabric scrap, 4" x 12"
Flat lace, ¼" wide, 20" (optional)
Sewing thread to match fabric and lace
Embroidery thread to match fabric, 20"
Very tiny safety pin

**1. Cutting and joining the pieces**—There are no patterns for the dress, since it is made entirely of straight pieces.

On the back of the fabric scrap, mark and cut two 4" x 6" pieces. Pin the two rectangles, right sides together, and stitch ¼" seams along each 4" edge, making each seam only 2¼" long. Leave open the remaining 1¾" for the arms. Press the seam allowance open, including the unstitched portions.

**2. Finishing the dress**—To make a hem along the lower edge of the unit, press 1" to the wrong side of the dress. Tuck under ¼" along the cut edge of the hem and stitch. If you wish, stitch lace to the lower edge of the dress and to the arm openings.

Along each top edge of the unit, press ½" to the wrong side and stitch ¼" casings, backstitching at the start and finish. Tie the embroidery thread (6 strands) to the safety pin and pull it through both casings.

Place the dress on the doll and pull the embroidery thread, adjusting the gathers evenly around the neck. Knot the thread securely at one shoulder, pull the thread ends to the inside of the dress, and trim. Slipstitch the arm openings to the doll.

## LONG CHRISTENING DRESS AND RUFFLED CAP
### Materials
Flat white eyelet lace, at least 6" wide, 24"
White batiste scrap, 14" x 14" (selvage along one edge)
White eyelet ruffle, about ⅞" wide including binding, 24"
White sewing thread
White ¼" fold-over bias tape, 20" (optional)
White embroidery thread, 20"
White ⅛" satin ribbon, 24"

**1. Cutting the pieces**—There are no patterns for the dress, since it is made entirely of straight pieces.

Cut the wide lace into two 6" x 7" pieces for the dress, reserving the remaining piece for the cap. Cut the batiste into two pieces for the slip, each 6" x 7". Place the selvage along one 7" edge of each piece. Cut two sleeves, each 2¾" x 3". Reserve the remaining batiste for the cap lining.

**2. Making the sleeves**—Fold a sleeve piece in half lengthwise, and finger-press it along the fold. Mark the center line with colored bastings. Remove the binding from a portion of the ⅞" eyelet ruffling to make a flat eyelet piece 3" long. Fold the lace in half lengthwise and press it, to indicate the center line.

Place the eyelet on top of the sleeve piece, right side up, matching the center line of the eyelet and the sleeve piece. Machine-stitch on the center line and along the unfinished edge of the lace. Remove the bastings.

Fold the sleeve in half crosswise, right sides together, and make a tube, by stitching a ¼″ seam along the entire 2¾″ edge. Turn the piece right side out and fold it to make a doubled sleeve, tucking the unfinished edge of the lace to the inside and aligning the two cut edges at the top. Baste the edges together. Repeat the procedure to make another sleeve and place them both on the baby.

**3. Preparing the dress and slip**—Stitch the two lace dress pieces, right sides together, making ¼″ side seams. Leave about 2″ open at the top of each seam for the arms. Press the unstitched seam allowance to the wrong side of the fabric. If you wish, bind the stitched portion of the seams.

Make the slip in the same way, leaving 2½″ open at the top of each seam for the arms. Place the selvage along the bottom edge. If desired, trim the bottom with the eyelet ruffling (which has had the binding removed). Fold under the unfinished edge of the lace and make two rows of machine stitches, to attach the lace and conceal the unfinished edge. If you wish, baste the seam allowances together and encase them in bias tape.

Turn the slip tube inside out and push it into the dress tube, positioning it so that the slip won't show below the scalloped edge of the dress. Hand-baste the lower edge. At the top of the unit, the slip will probably extend about ½″ beyond the dress. Baste together the slip and dress layers along the top, but don't baste the front and back together. Trim away the extra slip fabric. Working from the slip side of the unit, use tiny overcasting stitches to invisibly join the arm openings of the dress and slip. Remove the basting stitches along the bottom edge of the skirt. Press ½″ of each top edge to the slip side of the dress and then machine-stitch ¼″ casings, backstitching at the start and finish. Tie the length of white embroidery thread (6 strands) to a safety pin and pull it through the casing. Place the dress on the doll and pull the embroidery thread, adjusting the gathers evenly around the neck. Knot the thread securely at one shoulder. Pull the thread ends to the inside of the dress and trim them. Invisibly stitch the dress to the sleeves.

**4. Stitching the ruffled cap**—Complete the directions for the Basic Fabric Cap, using the flat embroidered eyelet for the outside of the cap and facing it with the batiste. Add eyelet ruffling to the front edge. Place the bound edge of the ruffle inside the cap and taper the lace toward each ribbon. Tack the excess eyelet on the inside.

## KNIT SHIRT
**Materials**
Knit fabric scrap, 7″ x 10″ (stripes horizontal to the long edge)
Sewing thread to match
Embroidery thread to match, 15″

**1. Making the shirt sleeves**—There are no patterns for the shirt, since it is made entirely of straight pieces.

On the back of the knit fabric, mark and cut out two 3″ x 4″ pieces for sleeves. Fold one piece in half lengthwise, right sides together, and make a tube, by stitching a ¼″ seam along the 4″ edge. Make a doubled sleeve, bringing the right side to the outside to meet the cut edges at the top. Baste the edges together. Pull the sleeve over the doll's arm and fold up a cuff. Repeat the procedure to make another sleeve.

**2. Completing the shirt**—From the remaining fabric, cut two 3¼″ x 4″ pieces for the shirt front and back. Pin the two pieces, right sides together, along the 3¼″ edges. Stitch ¼″ seams, making each seam only 1½″ long and leaving open the remaining 1¾″ for the arms. Press the seam allowances open, including the unstitched portions.

Make a ½″ hem along the lower edge. Along both top edges, press a ½″ hem to the wrong side and stitch ¼″ casings, backstitching at the start and finish. Tie the embroidery thread (6 strands) to the safety pin, and pull it through the two casings. Place the shirt on the baby and pull the embroidery thread, adjusting the gathers evenly around the neck. Knot the threads securely and tuck them inside the neckline. Overlap the cut edges of the sleeves with the shirt and slipstitch them together.

## SACQUE
### Materials
Flannel scrap, 4″ x 20″
Sewing thread to match
Contrasting embroidery thread, 2 yards
Very tiny safety pin

**1. Making the pattern**—Trace the sacque front pattern. The pattern lines are cutting lines. All the casings, hems, and ¼″ seam allowances are included.

**2. Cutting the fabric**—On the back of the flannel scrap, mark and cut out one sacque front and then flip the pattern over and mark one in reverse. Directly on the fabric, draw a 3″ x 6″ rectangle for the back of the sacque and two 3″ x 3¼″ pieces for the sleeves. Cut out all the pieces.

**3. Making the sleeves**—Fold one sleeve piece in half lengthwise, right sides together, and make a tube, by stitching a ¼″ seam along the open 3¼″ edge. Fold the piece to make a doubled sleeve, bringing the right side to the outside and aligning the cut edges at the top. Baste the edges together. Make tiny blanket stitches along the folded edges across the bottom of the sleeves, using two strands of thread. Repeat the procedure to make another sleeve, and place both on the baby. To do this with ease, stitch and tie a doubled thread to each of the doll's hands and then pull the knotted thread ends through the sleeves.

**4. Joining the front and back**—Pin the two sacque fronts to the sacque back, right sides together, with the curved front pieces overlapping at the center. Stitch ¼″ seams along each short edge, making each seam only 1¼″ long. Leave open the remaining 1¾″ for the arms. Press the seam allowances open, including the unstitched portions.

**5. Finishing the sacque**—To make a hem along the front and lower edge of the unit, baste a guideline of stitches ¼″ from the edges. Finger-press the hem to the wrong side, making a double-fold ⅛″ hem. Invisibly stitch it in place; then finish the front and lower edge with tiny blanket stitches.

Along each top edge of the unit, press ½″ to the wrong side of the sacque and stitch ¼″ casings, backstitching at the start and finish. Tie a 15″ length of embroidery thread (6 strands) to the safety pin and pull it through the casings.

Place the sacque on the baby and pull the embroidery thread, adjusting the gathers evenly around the neck. Knot the thread securely at the front, and tie the ends in a bow. Trim the thread ends and then knot them. Overlap the cut edges of the sleeves with the sacque and slipstitch them together.

## KNIT CAP
### Materials

One stretch-nylon toddler sock, size 4 to 5½,
  or 6″ x 7″ knit scrap
Sewing thread to match
Pom-pom, ½″ diameter

**1. Cutting the sock**—There is no pattern for
the sock cap.

Cut off the entire cuff area of the sock, just
above the heel. Turn the piece wrong side
out. The resulting tube should be about 3½″
long.

If using knit fabric, fold the right sides together lengthwise and stitch the long edge of
the tube.

**2. Stitching the cap**—Fold only the knit fabric to make a doubled cap, bringing the right
side to the outside and aligning the cut edges
at the top. By hand, make a line of running
stitches ¼″ from the cut edge of the sock or
the fabric. Pull the thread tightly to gather the
stitches, and then wrap the thread around the
fabric several times before knotting it. Turn
the cap right side out and stitch the pom-
pom to the top.

Place the cap on the baby and fold the finished edge once or twice to make a brim.
Invisibly stitch the cap to the doll's head.

## BONNET
### Materials

Fabric scrap, 7″ x 9″
Sewing thread to match
Satin ribbon, ⅛″ wide, 18″
Very tiny safety pin
Narrow lace, 8″ (optional)

**1. Making the pattern**—Trace the bonnet pattern from the book, copying all marks. The
pattern lines are cutting lines; ¼″ seam allowances are included.

**2. Cutting the fabric**—Make a trial bonnet
before you cut your good fabric. You may
need to adjust the pattern to fit your doll.

Fold the fabric in half lengthwise, right side
inside, and pin. Draw two bonnets, placing
the pattern on the fold where indicated. Cut
out each bonnet. Transfer the star, dots, and
casing lines to the wrong side of one bonnet
piece. Then transfer the casing lines to the
front of the piece, with basting stitches. On
the other bonnet piece, transfer only the star.

**3. Stitching the bonnet**—Lightly mark the
center back seam on each piece. Handling
each bonnet section separately (right side
folded to the inside), machine-stitch the center back, beginning at the star and tapering to
form a dart at the top fold. Backstitch at the
start and finish of each seam. Trim the seam
allowance to ⅛″, using pinking shears, or
trim and clip at intervals.

Turn one stitched bonnet section right side
out. Cup it inside the other section, right
sides together, to form a self-facing. Match up
the edges carefully. Machine-stitch the seam
along only the front curve of the brim, going
from white dot to white dot. Do not sew
across the casing opening. Trim the seam and
clip it, or use pinking shears.

Turn the bonnet right side out. Tuck under
the seam allowance along the back lower
edge and invisibly stitch it closed, still leaving the casing open. Press the brim so that
the seam is precisely on the edge, and then
baste it.

Machine-stitch the casing, backstitching at
the start and finish. Pull the ribbon through
the casing, using the tiny safety pin. Add lace
to the bonnet if you wish. Place the bonnet
on the baby and pull the ribbon ends, to
gather the bonnet around the face. Adjust the
fit before tying a bow, and invisibly stitch to
baby's head.

## BASIC FABRIC CAP
### Materials

Fabric scrap, 6¼″ square
Sewing thread to match
Satin ribbon, ⅛″ wide, 18″
Very tiny safety pin
Narrow lace, 8″ (optional)

**1. Making the pattern**—Trace the pattern and
the dots. The pattern lines are the cutting
lines; ¼″ seam allowances are included.

**2. Cutting the fabric**—Make a trial cap before you cut your good fabric. You may need
to adjust the pattern to fit your doll.

Fold the square of fabric in half, right side
inside, and pin. Lightly draw two caps, with
dots, placing the pattern on the fold where
indicated. Cut out the two pieces.

**3. Stitching the cap**—Open each cap section
flat, and then press and baste each neck-edge
seam allowance to the wrong side. Handling

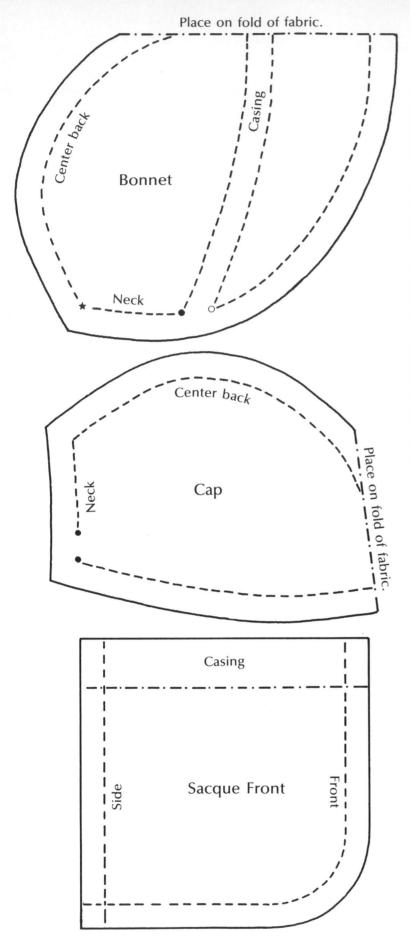

Place on fold of fabric.

Center back

Casing

Bonnet

Neck

Center back

Neck

Cap

Place on fold of fabric.

Casing

Side

Sacque Front

Front

each cap section separately, fold the right side to the inside and machine-stitch the center back seam, tapering to form a dart at the top fold. Trim the seam to ⅛" and clip it at intervals, or use pinking shears.

Turn one stitched cap section right side out. To form a self-facing, cup it inside the other section, so that the right sides are together. Machine-stitch the seam along the long front edge, trim it to ⅛", and clip it.

Turn the cap right side out and close the opening with invisible stitches. Leave open the ¼" area between the dots, for a casing. Press the cap front so that the seam is precisely on the edge, and then baste.

Machine-stitch a casing, ¼" from the front edge, backstitching at the start and finish. Pull the ribbon through the casing, using the tiny safety pin. Place the cap on the baby and pull the ribbon ends, to gather the cap front edge. Adjust the fit before tying a bow. Trim the front edge of the cap with lace, if you wish, and invisibly stitch the cap to the doll's head.

# HOLLY BEARIES

A Holly Beary is a cooperative little Christmas creature, which you mold and fold and then stitch to stay in a sitting, standing, sleeping, or climbing position. You can attach the head so that it faces straight forward, or you can position it so that the face looks to the left or to the right. You may think of the Holly Beary as just an ornament, but there are many ways it can entertain you.

Just as they are, the bears make perfect little tree ornaments, but they're even cuter when they carry tiny ornaments of their own, such as bells or baskets or wreaths.

# A PAIR OF LIVELY LIONS

*Bathtime isn't such a big chore when this father and son team do the lion's share of work. These mitts are designed to make bathtime fun for little scrubbers.*

*You can make these washcloth puppets in two sizes—one that's big enough for a grown-up helper, and a smaller one that is cub-sized.*

**Materials** *(for one mitt, either size)*
Two honey-colored borderless velour wash-
   cloths
Sewing thread: honey, cream
Cream grosgrain ribbon, 3" long: lion, 1"
   wide; cub, ⅝" wide
Embroidery thread: 1½ yards each, cream,
   peach, brown
Cream pregathered crochet-type lace, 18":
   lion, 1½" wide; cub, ⅞" wide

**1. Making the pattern**—To make a complete pattern for either size puppet, draw the lion of your choice on a folded piece of tracing paper and cut it out. The pattern line is the stitching line for each puppet. To make a template of the pattern, cut out the eyes, triangular nose, and cheeks. Then use a large needle to pierce the embroidery lines for the mouth and whiskers and the placement lines for the nose strip and the mane.

**2. Preparing the mitt front**—For either size mitt front, pin the pattern to the terry side of a washcloth, placing the lower edge of the pattern along the finished edge of the cloth. Trace the pattern outline with a vanishing fabric marker. Baste around the outline, to transfer the lion shape to the velour side.

Now repin the pattern to the velour side of the cloth, placing it within the basted outline, and use a vanishing fabric marker to lightly draw the facial details and the placement lines for the nose strip and the mane.

To attach the grosgrain nose strip, tuck under ¼" of one cut end of the proper width ribbon and pin it in place on the face, over-lapping the seam allowance at the top of the head. The folded end of the ribbon should rest on the top of the triangular nose. Appli-qué the folded and finished edges by hand or machine, stitching both sides of the ribbon in the same direction.

**3. Embroidering the face**—For either the lion or the cub, use brown embroidery thread (1 strand) to chain-stitch the nose and the mouth lines. Satin-stitch (2 strands) peach cheeks and a brown nose and eyes, and use cream thread (2 strands) to chain-stitch the whiskers. Pull out the basting stitches if the vanishing fabric marker outline is still visible.

**4. Joining the front and back**—Lay the em-broidered mitt front face down on the velour or terry side (whichever you prefer) of a sec-ond washcloth, aligning the finished edges along the bottom. Pin and baste the layers to-gether and machine-stitch around the outline. Backstitch at the start and finish and leave the bottom open.

Cut out the lion shape, leaving a ¼" seam allowance. Grade the seam allowance by trimming one edge (either the front or the back) to ⅛". Clip around the curves and into the V-shaped areas at the neck and ears, but don't clip the seams.

Turn the mitt right side out, gently pushing out the curved areas. Hand-press each mitt flat, making sure that the seam is exactly on the edge. Pin the front and back together and machine-topstitch around the edge of the mitt, leaving the bottom open. To define the head, topstitch along the base of each ear.

**5. Adding the mane**—Place your hand inside the mitt and hand-stitch the pregathered lace mane to the head, using the 1½"-wide lace for the lion and the ⅞"-wide lace for the cub. Begin by stitching the lace behind the ear. Following the placement line, invisibly stitch the mane around the face, behind the other ear, and along the top of the head. Join the cut ends of the lace behind the first ear.

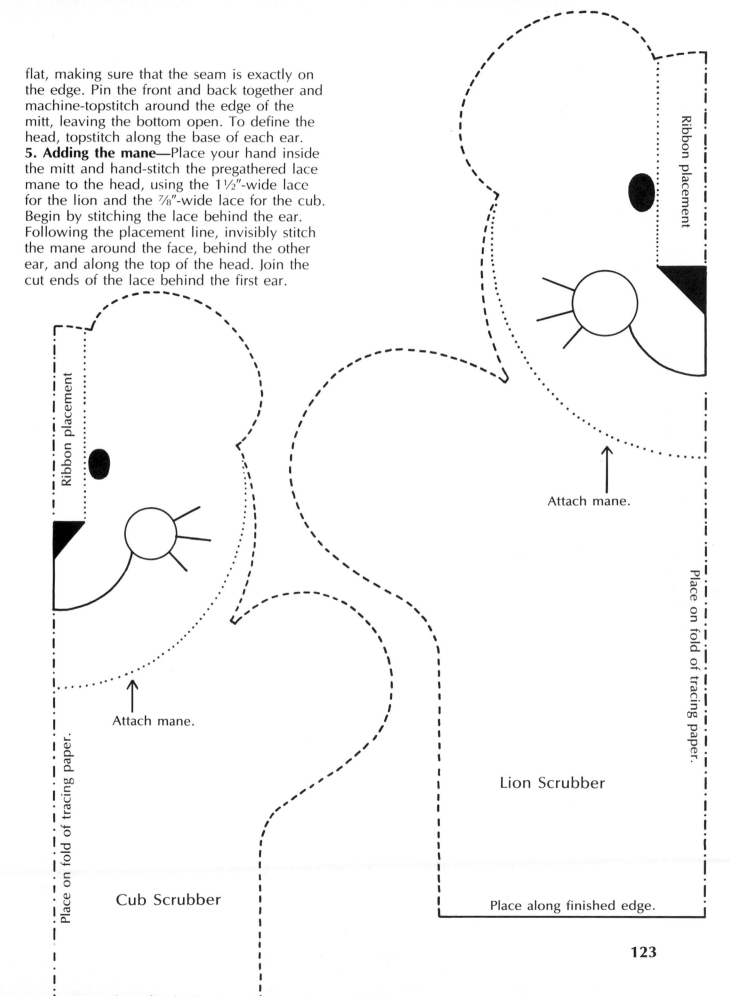

Ribbon placement

Attach mane.

Lion Scrubber

Place on fold of tracing paper.

Place along finished edge.

Ribbon placement

Attach mane.

Cub Scrubber

Place on fold of tracing paper.

Place along finished edge.

# O CHRISTMAS TREE

'Tis the season to be sewing—ornaments for the tree. A Christmas sampler of ornament types and techniques is offered in this chapter, so you can stitch and stuff fabric, appliqué felt, weave ribbon, embroider, or crochet.

Because the earliest Christmas trees were decorated with candles and edible ornaments, a "recipe" is included for some embroidered Felt Cookie Ornaments that have a fantastic shelf-life! There are tiny Ruffled Wreaths to stitch in a zip. Of course, Santa must make an appearance. He stars as an ornament and a tree-topper, too.

For even more inspiration, flip back through the pages of the book and borrow designs for ornaments from other chapters. Create a whole choir of angels, or some little lambs using the patterns from the Crèche in Chapter One, or borrow the symbols from the Advent Window Banner in the same chapter. The Miniature Chairs in Chapter Two and the Mice in Chapter Three would also be perfect ornaments.

# GIFT PACKAGE TREE SKIRT

*Even before Santa arrives, you can surround your tree with holiday gift packages, fashioned from Christmas scraps and grosgrain ribbons. Or try combining just a few Christmas fabrics with other red-and-green prints, stripes, and checks. If your scraps are small, piece them together under the ribbons, as I did.*

*After you clear away the opened gifts, freshen the flattened bows on the tree skirt with a curling iron. When you store the skirt, stuff tissue paper into each ribbon loop, and the bows will look perky when you unpack the skirt next year.*

**Materials**

White opaque fabric, 36" x 36"
Print or solid fabric for backing, 36" x 36"
Quilt batting, 36" x 70" (36" circle, eight 11" squares)
Four different green prints, each 11" x 22"
Four different red prints, each 11" x 22"
Sewing thread: white, green, red
White ¼" fold-over bias tape, 4½ yards
Washable 1" grosgrain ribbon: 4½ yards green, 4½ yards red
Hook-and-eye fasteners, five small sets

**1. Making the patterns**—Trace the pattern for the gift package on folded paper, copying the ribbon placement lines. The ¼" seam allowances are included. Cut out the pattern. Use a large needle to pierce the ribbon placement lines.

Draw a circle with a 35½" diameter and a 4" center opening for the tree-skirt base pattern. Refer to Step 1 of the Christmas Memories Tree Skirt on page 145 for directions.

**2. Marking and cutting the fabrics**—On the large white fabric square, mark the skirt base and the center opening, but don't cut out the skirt yet. Mark the quarter sections with a vanishing fabric marker. Don't bother to mark the batting or the backing fabric at this time.

To make the packages, fold each printed scrap in half crosswise, right side on the outside, and pin the layers together. Trace a gift package on each scrap and then cut out the square. Use a vanishing fabric marker or a light pencil to indicate the ribbon placement lines on one square of each print.

Cut a 36" square of batting and reserve it for the tree-skirt base. From the remaining batting, cut eight 11" squares for the gift packages.

**3. Preparing the skirt base**—On a large flat surface, spread out the square of backing fabric, right side down. Add the large batting square. Finally, add the circle-marked white fabric, right side up. Smooth out the wrinkles and pin all the layers together. Securely baste around the large circular outline and around the center-opening outline. Stitch very close to the outlines within the skirt area. Use basting stitches to indicate the quarter sections. This will prevent the fabric layers from shifting and will help you to place the packages accurately.

With pins in place, machine-stitch around the skirt and around the center opening. Both lines of stitches should be within the skirt area, ⅛" from the outlines.

Decide which of the quarter-section lines will be the back opening. Make a row of machine stitches ⅛" on each side of the line. Cut out the large circle, following the outline. Then cut up toward the center, on the line between the two rows of stitching. Cut out the center opening.

Use the bias tape to encase the cut edges of the skirt base, following the manufacturer's directions. Set the skirt base aside.

**4. Making a gift package**—From the green grosgrain ribbon, cut five strips the following lengths: two pieces, each 10½" long; two pieces, each 8" long; and one piece 2" long. Baste one 10½" length within the ribbon placement lines on the right side of one of the red packages. Machine-stitch both edges of the ribbon in the same direction. Baste and stitch the second 10½" length in place, crossing over the first ribbon.

To make the gift-package back, use a matching unmarked red square and pin and baste it, right side up, to a batting square.

Pin the gift-package back to the beribboned square, right sides together. Machine-stitch the edges, leaving a 3" opening along one edge for turning. Trim the batting, clip off the corners, and turn the piece right side out. Close the opening with invisible hand

# WOVEN-RIBBON HEART BASKETS

*A traditional Swedish paper ornament was the inspiration for these woven-ribbon heart baskets. The satin ornament can easily be tucked inside a Christmas card and sent on its way with love.*

*The first time you read through the directions you might think, "I can't do that!" But you'll be pleasantly surprised, if you give it a try. Make the first ornament when you're fresh and able to concentrate. Once you understand the technique, you'll be able to weave the baskets very quickly.*

**Materials** *(for one ornament)*
White satin ribbon, 1½" wide, 9";
  ⅜" wide, ¾ yard
Red or green satin ribbon: 1½" wide, 9";
  ⅜" wide, 1 yard
A small quantity of polyester stuffing
Sewing thread to match the ribbon colors

**1. Drawing the pattern**—Trace the pattern for the heart top and cut it out. The straight edge of the pattern is meant to be placed against the finished edge of the wide ribbon. The curved edge of the pattern is the stitching line for the heart top.

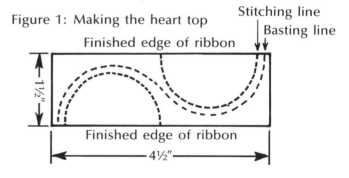

Figure 1: Making the heart top

Stitching line
Basting line
Finished edge of ribbon
1½"
Finished edge of ribbon
4½"

**2. Making the heart top**—Cut the 1½"-wide white ribbon into two 4½" pieces. Referring to Figure 1, line up the straight edge of the pattern directly along one finished ribbon edge, on the dull side of the ribbon. Use a sharp soft pencil to draw around the curved edge of the pattern. Then draw a second heart top along the opposite edge of the same ribbon piece, but don't cut the ribbon at this time.

Baste the shiny sides of the two ribbon pieces together, as shown in Figure 1. Then make small machine stitches on the curved pattern lines, backstitching at the start and finish. Add ⅛" seam allowances as you cut out each heart top. Use pinking shears, if possible, or use scissors and clip around the curve at close intervals.

Turn the heart tops right side out and press

carefully. Repeat the above procedure, using the 1½"-wide colored ribbon. Leave all the straight edges open.

**3. Preparing and attaching the ribbon strips**—From the ⅜"-wide white ribbon, cut five strips, each 4½" long. On the dull side of the five ribbons, lightly pencil a ¼" seam allowance at each cut end.

Figure 2: Attaching the ribbons

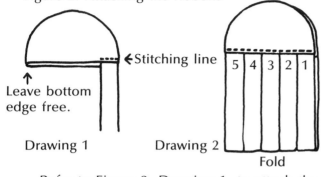

Drawing 1          Drawing 2

Refer to Figure 2, Drawing 1, to attach the ribbon strips to the heart tops. Insert one cut end of one of the narrow white ribbon strips, dull side up, into one white heart top piece. Place the pencil line of the strip against the finished edge of the heart top. Join the strip to one edge of the heart top, leaving the edge behind the strip free. Make tiny hand stitches, placing them close to the finished edge of the ribbon, and then knot the thread. Add the four remaining white strips in the same way. Now turn the work over so that the shiny sides of the strips are up, and close the open edge of the heart top, inserting a little stuffing into the heart top before you stitch it closed. Repeat the procedure to attach the opposite ends of the white ribbon strips to the remaining white heart top.

Follow these directions to make a similar unit, using the colored heart tops and the colored narrow ribbon. Reserve a piece of colored narrow ribbon for the handle.

**4. Weaving the basket**—Position the white ribbon unit, shiny side up. Fold the unit in half, as in Figure 2, Drawing 2, shiny side out. Press the center fold. Fold the colored ribbon unit in the same way.

To weave the first row of the basket, refer to Figure 3, Drawing 1. Place the white unit in your left hand and the colored unit in your right hand, with the heart tops pointing away from you. Hold the units at right angles to each other. Weave together, inserting the first

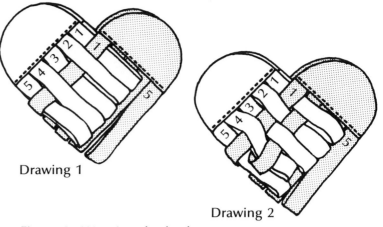

Drawing 1

Drawing 2

Figure 3: Weaving the basket

white strip through the first colored strip. Then insert that first colored strip through the second white strip. Insert the third white strip through the first colored strip. Insert the first colored strip through the fourth white strip and insert the fifth white strip inside the first colored strip.

Push the completed row toward the white heart top. Refer to Figure 3, Drawing 2, to weave the second row. Insert the second colored strip through the first white strip and then insert the second white strip through the second colored strip. Insert the second colored strip through the third white strip. Insert the fourth white strip through the second colored strip and insert the second colored strip through the fifth white strip.

Repeat these steps to weave the remaining three rows, alternating the color of the starting strip. The basket will look neat and flat when completed.

**5. The finishing touches**—Make a few invisible stitches to hold the ribbon layers together and to strengthen the basket. Stitch at the center top of the heart on both the front and the back of the basket. Stitch again on each side edge of the basket, where the weaving ends and the heart top begins.

To make the handle, cut the remaining colored ribbon to an 8" length. Fold ¼" of each cut end toward the shiny side of the ribbon. Invisibly stitch the handle to the inside of the basket.

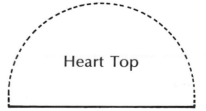

Place along finished edge of ribbon.

# SANTA STAR

*For many children, Santa Claus is the superstar of Christmas. So here he is—presented as Santa Star!*

*Two patterns are provided, so that Santa can be given top billing in place of the traditional star, or play a minor role as an ornament on a lower branch of your tree.*

**Materials for Ornament**
Red felt, 5" x 11"
White felt, 2" x 3"
Pink felt, 2" x 3"
Black felt, 3" x 3"
Embroidery thread: 36" red; 18" each, black, white, light pink, medium pink
Polyester stuffing
White ¼" crochet-type lace, 6"
White ball fringe, ½" diameter or less
Gold thread or cord, 5"

**Materials for Tree Topper**
Red felt, 10" x 18"
White felt, 3" x 5"
Pink felt, 3" x 4"
Black felt, 5" x 5"
Embroidery thread: 1½ yards red; 1 yard each, black, white, light pink, medium pink
Polyester stuffing
White ½" crochet-type lace, 10"
White ball fringe, ¾" diameter
Red ribbon, ¼" or ⅜" wide, 24"

**1. Making the patterns**—Trace and cut out the patterns for the ornament or the tree topper. Copy all the lines and the details on the body and the face. Use a large needle to pierce the embroidery lines. To make a template of the face pattern, cut the features with a craft knife.

**2. Marking and cutting the felt**—On a single layer of red felt, mark two star body pieces. Use a sharp pencil to lightly transfer the placement and topstitching lines on each, but draw the buttons and beard placement lines on only one of the pieces.

On the white felt, mark one beard and one back hair piece. Draw four hands and one face on the pink felt, lightly transferring the features. Also mark four black boots. Cut out all the pieces on the pattern lines; no seam allowances are needed.

**3. Making the Santa front**—Use the tiniest drops of fabric glue to attach the face to the beard and then stick the beard to the star body, applying a small amount of glue under the face area only. The beard below the face should be free.

Use a single strand of embroidery thread for all the stitchery on the ornament and two strands for the tree topper. Blanket-stitch all the edges of the face, using the light pink thread. Use red to backstitch the mouth and satin-stitch the nose. Make black satin stitches for the tree topper eyes and black straight stitches for the ornament's eyes. Use medium pink satin stitches for the cheeks. Use white to satin-stitch the buttons and edge the beard with blanket stitches. Make sure the beard is not attached to the body.

Glue the hands in place and use light pink blanket stitches to appliqué the edges bordering the sleeves. Attach the boots and appliqué the edges, bordering the pants with black blanket stitches.

**4. Appliquéing the Santa back**—Glue the back hair in place and blanket-stitch both long edges with white thread. Also attach the hands and boots and edge these with matching blanket stitches, as described in Step 3.

**5. Joining the front and back**—Pin the Santa front and back, wrong sides together. Stuff the legs and close the edges of the legs with blanket stitches, matching the thread and felt colors. Stitch and stuff the arms in the same manner. Use red thread to topstitch the lines that define the body. Keep the lines straight, by turning the work as you pass the needle from one side to the other. Stuff the head area and blanket-stitch the opening closed.

**6. Adding the finishing touches**—To border the hat and sleeves, stitch the lace in place. Securely tack a ball fringe to the hat peak. For the ornament, add a gold thread or cord hanging loop behind the ball fringe. For the tree topper, stitch two 12" lengths of ribbon near the arm folds on the back of Santa, so that he can be tied to the top of the tree.

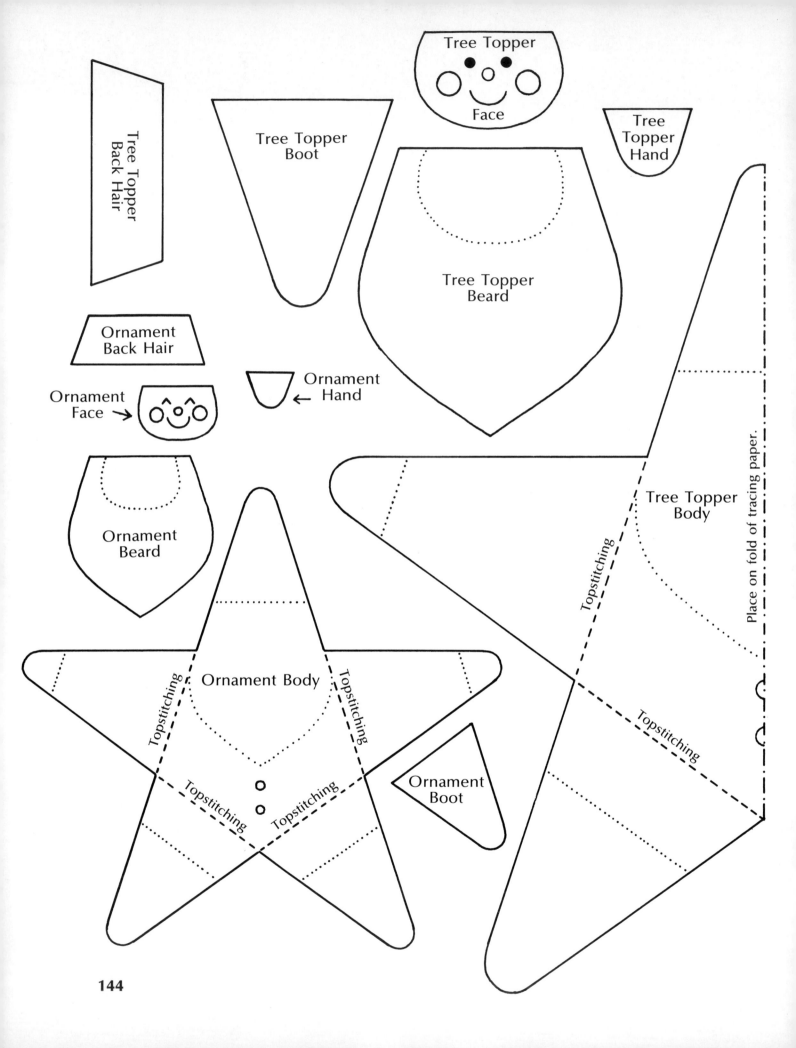

Tree Topper
Back Hair

Tree Topper
Boot

Tree Topper
Face

Tree
Topper
Hand

Tree Topper
Beard

Ornament
Back Hair

Ornament
Hand

←

Ornament
Face →

Ornament
Beard

Tree Topper
Body

Place on fold of tracing paper.

Topstitching

Topstitching

Ornament Body

Topstitching

Topstitching

Topstitching

Topstitching

Topstitching

Ornament
Boot

144

# CHRISTMAS MEMORIES TREE SKIRT

*A parade of Christmas memories marches around this ruffled tree skirt. The twenty-four symbols are borrowed from the Advent Window Banner. Perhaps you would like to add treasured symbols of your own to this collection of motifs, or you might consider using only one or a few of the symbols and repeating them around the skirt.*

**Materials**
White opaque fabric, 36" x 36"
Green fabric, 36" x 36"
Red print fabric, 1⅛ yards
Green-and-white striped fabric, ¾ yard
Washable green felt, three pieces, each
 8½" x 11"
Green ¼" fold-over bias tape, 16 yards
Sewing thread: green, red
Quilt batting, 36" x 36"
Green embroidery thread, 20 yards

**1. Making the patterns**—Trace the patterns for the Christmas symbols on pages 31, 32, and 33. They are the same symbols used for the Advent Window Banner.

To make each of the two circle patterns, it's easiest to draw one quarter section of each circle. Then trace three more same-size sections, and tape all four sections together to make a complete pattern. Cut it out.

The diameter of the largest circle is 35½". Since you're making a quarter section of the

# HOLIDAY SNOWMEN

*Like folded paper cutouts, lines of chubby little snowmen link arms to cheerfully border these holiday hostess aprons, the perfect attire for your Christmas tree-trimming party. Use a single snowman to add a whimsical touch to an appliquéd bib or as a cute ornament to decorate your tree.*

*For practicality, all the materials you select must be washable. Although the felt you purchase may claim to be machine washable and dryable, its surface will not remain pretty if the aprons make too many trips to the laundry. No matter what the label says, I would never machine-wash or tumble-dry the work. Delicate hand washing in cool water with mild soap is best.*

### SNOWMAN APRONS
**Materials for Small Child Size**
Red quilted fabric, 17" x 17"
Washable white felt, 8" x 17"
Washable black felt, 4" x 8½"
Embroidery thread: 1½ yards red, 4 yards
   black
Green ½" fold-over bias tape, 4 yards
Washable ⅜" metallic striped ribbon, 45"
Sewing thread: green, white, black

**Materials for Large Child Size**
Red quilted fabric, 17" x 22"
Washable white felt, 9" x 17"
Washable black felt, 4" x 8½"
Embroidery thread: 1½ yards red, 4 yards
   black
Green ½" fold-over bias tape, 4¼ yards
Washable ⅜" metallic striped ribbon, 45"
Sewing thread: green, white, black

**Materials for Adult Size**
Red quilted fabric, 23" x 30"
Washable white felt, 13" x 23"
Washable black felt, 9" x 10"
Embroidery thread: 4 yards red, 6 yards black
Green ½" fold-over bias tape, 6½ yards
Washable ⅝" metallic striped ribbon, 52"
Sewing thread: green, white, black

**1. Making the patterns**—Make a grid of 1"
squares to match the grid in Figure 1. Select
the size apron you want to make. Enlarge the
half-pattern in the book on your grid, following the directions in Supplies & Techniques.
   Trace the snowman and hat patterns (large
for adult apron, small for children's aprons).
Cut out the eyes, cheeks, and buttons and
pierce the mouth dots and hat placement
lines to make a template of the snowman.
The pattern lines will be the cutting lines. To

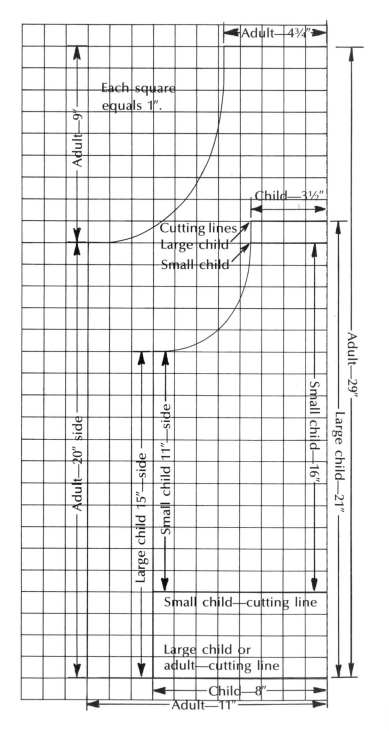